CHASING EDEN

Books by Howard Mansfield

Cosmopolis
In the Memory House
Skylark
The Same Ax, Twice
The Bones of the Earth
Turn & Jump
Dwelling in Possibility
Sheds
Summer Over Autumn
The Habit of Turning the World Upside Down

Editor

Where the Mountain Stands Alone

For Children

Hogwood Steps Out

HOWARD MANSFIELD

CHASING EDEN

A BOOK OF SEEKERS

Bauhan Publishing · Peterborough · New Hampshire
2021

Library of Congress Cataloging-in-Publication Data:
Names: Mansfield, Howard, author.
Title: Chasing Eden : a book of seekers / Howard Mansfield.
Description: Peterborough, New Hampshire : Bauhan Publishing, 2021. |
    Includes bibliographical references.
Identifiers: LCCN 2021028141 (print) | LCCN 2021028142 (ebook) | ISBN
    9780872333505 (trade paperback) | ISBN 9780872333512 (ebook)
Subjects: LCSH: National characteristics, American--History. | American
    Dream. | Utopias--United States. | Pilgrims and pilgrimages--United
    States. | United States--Religion. | United States--Civilization.
Classification: LCC E169.1 .M2565 2021 (print) | LCC E169.1 (ebook) | DDC
    973--dc23
LC record available at https://lccn.loc.gov/2021028141
LC ebook record available at https://lccn.loc.gov/2021028142

Book design by Sarah Bauhan.
Cover design by Henry James.
Cover painting: *Saco River* by Benjamin Champney, Courtesy of the New
Hampshire Historical Society. Used by permission. www.nhhistory.org
Howard can be reached at www.howardmansfield.com

BAUHAN
PUBLISHING LLC
PO BOX 117 PETERBOROUGH NEW HAMPSHIRE 03458
603-567-4430
WWW.BAUHANPUBLISHING.COM

Printed in the United States of America

Once again, and always, for Dr. B. A. Millmoss

"All history is the history of longing."

—Jackson Lears, historian, 2009

"Every force evolves a form."

—Oliver C. Hampton, Shaker elder, 1892

CONTENTS

INTRODUCTION

Seekers

The Mummyjums making their pilgrimage were a sight. Dressed in bearskins and rags with "a very short staff in each hand . . . they were obliged to walk with their bodies bent in a horizontal position, which with their long beards, odd grimaces, incoherent language, and singular maneuvers, gave them a very ludicrous appearance," said one observer. They often repeated the same expressions rapidly, such as "My God, my God, my God, my God, my God, what wouldst thou have me to do?—Mummyjum, mummyjum, mummyjum, mummyjum, mummyjum."

Their prophet, Isaac Bullard, had left Canada with a band of eight, including his wife and child, after being tried and acquitted for the death of an infant. He landed in Woodstock, Vermont, in 1817. Vermont, already shaken by evangelical revivals and breakaway sects, was upset in the aftermath of "the Year without Summer," known also as "eighteen hundred and froze to death." It snowed in June (six inches near Woodstock; eighteen inches farther north). Crops failed, farms failed. Newly shorn sheep died. Drought followed the cold. People were desperate for salvation. They deserted the old churches for the Baptist New Lights, Methodist camp meetings, and small bands of believers of one or two dozen who prayed without ceasing, and ceased.

The Mummyjums fasted constantly and ate meagerly, usually gruel of mush and milk or flour mixed with water, which they sucked up with a cane stalk from a communal trough while standing up. They would pray by throwing themselves face-first into the dirt and rolling around. They never changed their clothes, bathed, or cut their hair. Wretchedness was the key to the kingdom. Their prophet, they boasted, had worn the same rags for seven years. They were weak, dirty, and infested with lice and smallpox. Even so, two Shaker villages along their route offered them food and shelter, only to be vilified by Bullard and his followers. Every word the Shakers spoke "was of the Devil," they said.

But such extremism did not isolate the Mummyjums. In Vermont, Bullard gathered forty converts, including a Methodist minister and his family. They became known as the Vermont Pilgrims, and they set out for the Promised Land. Bullard divined their pilgrimage route each morning by throwing down his staff. It always pointed southwest, it was said.

As they walked, these "wretched fanaticks" made news. In some places, thousands turned out to see them. The reports, no matter the place, were uniform: "as filthy a horde of beings as can possibly be imagined" with "the most nauseous stench." The prophet Bullard berated his audiences, saying that terrible misfortune would befall them if they didn't join his pilgrims. "Hell and damnation, hell and damnation is your portion if you don't repent," he said. At other times he was incoherent. "The old prophet was then groaning M-O-O-H! M-O-O-H! with an emphatic motion of the right hand and body, and which came from his hoarse throat, like the bellowing of a bull," reported one witness. The mayor of Cincinnati, concerned about the spread of smallpox, asked that they camp a mile from the city. By this point, Bullard had gathered as many as fifty-five disciples who had forsaken all worldly property to obediently follow their prophet's every utterance and gesture. He was an absolute ruler.

They sold their wagons and horses and bought a flatboat to ride the Ohio River to the Mississippi and on to the Promised Land. Sickness, death, and desertion followed. Their numbers dwindled. They camped on an island in the Mississippi near the small town of Little Prairie, Missouri. The island was known for many years after this as Pilgrim

Island. Here, sick and starving, as many as thirty to forty Pilgrims died. Bullard, following a revelation, ordered that they not bury their dead. A visitor saw the bones "bleaching" in the sun. A few of his followers escaped and made their way back to join the Shakers. The county sheriff landed and, holding off the adults with his sword, fed the starving children. Boatmen landed and robbed the Mummyjums of whatever they had to rob, which couldn't have been much. Another crew landed and forcibly washed Bullard, cutting off his long red beard.

The Mummyjums were last seen in 1825, eight years since they had set out from Vermont. Only two women remained on an island, dressed in rags, living in a hut of reeds, bark, and boards. Bullard had vanished, his death unrecorded. A visitor offered to pay their passage back to Cincinnati so they could return to their native New England. No, they said, "nothing on earth would induce them to leave." They had found the Promised Land.

The Mummyjums were dirty and crazy, and yet essential to the American experience. They didn't just "follow their bliss." They were in hot pursuit. As strange as they were, they are familiar. Had they wandered into the California of the 1960s, Joan Didion might have written about them. They could have been living in a canyon not far from the Manson family.

Their story was not uncommon in the nineteenth century. There were new religions, revivals, a "Great Awakening," prophets and Messiahs everywhere: Mormons, Oneida Perfectionists, Swedenborgians, Christian Connexion, Christian Scientists, Theosophists, Disciples of Christ, Millerites, who preached that the end of the world was coming by 1844, and many smaller sects like Janssonists, vegetarian Dorrilites, New Thought, the Halcyon Empire, Publick Universal Friend, and the "dancing Johnites," who followed their prophet as he rode a painted horse declaring that he was St. John the Divine. When they crossed paths in upstate New York, the Mummyjums won converts among the dancing Johnites. The earliest of these movements, "Shakers, Universalists, and Freewill Baptists gave first voice to the many for whom life in America must always proclaim a revolution of the spirit," says scholar Stephen A. Marini.

There were many experimenters in the land. Americans were once full of the mad energy of Utopianists, as if they were convulsed by the falling away of boundaries, driven crazy with possibility. They produced an astonishing array of utopias, almost at the rate Ford once rolled new models and styles off the assembly line, new ideas about sharing property, work, and love.

"We are all a little wild here with numberless projects of social reform. Not a reading man but has a draft of a new Community in his waistcoat pocket," Ralph Waldo Emerson wrote to Thomas Carlyle in 1840. "One man renounces the use of animal food; and another of coin; and another of domestic hired service; and another of the State; and on the whole we have a commendable share of reason and hope." Emerson's own friends were planning an experimental commune. "I am gently mad myself, and am resolved to live cleanly," said Emerson, but he would not join. His close friend Henry David Thoreau would conduct his own experiment in living, moving into his cabin at Walden Pond on Independence Day in 1845.

Some of these beliefs overtook society. They were not just the concerns of a strange cavalcade of ragged pilgrims or communards who had removed themselves. Spiritualism, the belief that we can communicate with the dead, was the talk of the 1850s. It was allied with the reform movements for abolition, temperance, and women's rights. Almost all the leading abolitionists were Spiritualists. Many Americans went to séances and were fascinated by the Fox sisters, two girls from a small town in upstate New York who produced the sounds of the dead "rapping" in response to their questions. There were many willing believers. Few dismissed this rapping outright or the floating and turning tables at séances. Often they looked for other explanations such as electricity—the new force summoned to explain everything—

or even the recently imagined "Odic force." They sought empirical proof for the spirit realm.

The spirits usually spoke of mundane things, which was proof of the spirit life, said the Spiritualists. To Emerson and Thoreau, it was all just a heap of metaphysical Barnum—"the Rat-revelation, the Gospel that comes by taps in the wall," said Emerson. If this rapping is what the next life offers, said Thoreau, "exchange my immortality for a glass of cold beer."

The Shakers, who sometimes saw angels, were right in time with Spiritualist America. The belief in "spirit messages" was so widespread that clergy and newspapers denounced séances as an invitation for Satan to come calling. By the 1870s, Spiritualism was waning.

This spiritual hunger was part of the chaotic churning of nineteenth-century America, with its frenzied railroad construction, land speculators, deadly labor strikes, riots, hucksters, immigrants, slavers, and slave catchers; Civil War and three foreign wars; pioneers burning forests and prairies, exterminating the buffalo and the Indians as they went; reformers of schools, prisons, housing, hospitals, asylums, poorhouses, factories, cemeteries, city sanitation, and village life. America in the nineteenth century was consumed by many fevers all at once.

Our agitation has not ceased; it has taken different forms. At any time there are five hundred thousand people in the air, thirty thousand feet up over France, California, Japan, the vast reaches of the Pacific. Six million people a day in flight. There were 4.3 billion air travelers in 2018, which is forecast to nearly double to 7.8 billion in 2036, says the International Air Transport Association. Millions more are traveling by rail, bus, car, ship, and foot. Air terminals, railway stations, ports, and roads are filled with tourists, travelers, voyagers, sojourners, pilgrims. What are we looking for in this "gadding about," as one nineteenth-century curmudgeon said, in all this ceaseless hurry? Many people are going to work, of course, going home, doing what they have done time and again. And many more, some unknowingly, are on a quest looking for *something*, "out of the cradle, endlessly rocking," as Walt Whitman said.

～

We usually tell the American story of seekers and pilgrims by going to the end of the road. We follow the Mummyjums to their island ending. The end of the road beckons. Some years ago we were in San Francisco, released from a New Hampshire winter into the Pacific sunshine, swimming in colors and light unknown back east. My wife and I poured over the personals in the *San Francisco Bay Guardian*, dramas bursting beyond their few lines. Under the heading "Crossed Signals":

"12/11. Highway 80! Afternoon. Me: Mercedes. You: Saab wagon. You waved, we smiled. I exited after the Bridge. I want to meet!"

And: "Cindy, Wu Li girl at Café Med, 12/6. Wonderful discourse concerning Taoism, anti-oxidants, synchronicity, physics, philosopher stones, etc."

"Etc.?" How much more can you cram into one "discourse?" We headed south on the Pacific Coast Highway, driving through many weathers, fogs of different hue and heft. Some were like gray fabric, some thin, some backlit as the sun burned them off. In places, the coastal fog parted, revealing the blue just beyond, the silver-green hills, the bright yellows and browns, all framed by the fog as if we were looking out of a tunnel. Each twist and curl of the two-lane road revealed the land in a new light.

We were headed to Deetjen's Big Sur Inn, a funky collection of twenty small cabins in the redwoods. Our room, on the second floor of a cabin, had views into the trees. We could hear a creek running. Deetjens seemed like it was built on a whim, and like some adult might arrive at any minute to order us to take down these treehouses and snug clubhouses.

In our room were notebooks, some with flowery covers, with guests' responses to the place. ("I love it here because I'm here with

Kyle and Kyle loves me.") In the most recent notebook, J. B. writes, epigrammatically, "As if I were an ornament on a Christmas tree perceiving." Under that, the rest, three-quarters of the page, is blank. On another page, Rachel from Massachusetts confides, "Dear Dan and Bob, I hope you're reading this because you'll know why I changed. . . . This place will be my home now, I can't wait to get home again, again and again. Please remember me, Big Sur, I will be back to ask questions and I'll bring my family."

It's hard to stop reading these inscriptions once you start. It's like snooping in someone else's drawers. The messages veer from public announcement to intimate confession to snapshots of a mind circling itself. Some say simply: thank you, beautiful place, we enjoyed our stay. Others write that they are "healing a broken heart" in finding their first night of peaceful sleep. "In this place, at any age, one has the feeling that dreams can still come true." And: "The Great Spirit can hug you here."

Page after page. Searchers after peace, joy, humility, love, God, a good meal paired with the right wine, a "comfy-cozy bed." Here, at the continent's edge, the seekers have found, like so many before them, that there is no further to go.

At dinner in Deetjen's small, cottage-like dining rooms, a man is talking urgently about a mystic. He is pedantic about it. Maybe because he is traveling alone, his words rush forth out of hours of silence—a horse breaking from the starting gate. Or maybe this is why he is alone. He doesn't listen to a word the host, a woman in her forties with short blond hair, says. He insists on every point. (My apologies to the millions of Californians who are not mystic-manqués. California is the world's fifth largest economy, so there have to be people who just go to work and then to their kids' soccer games.)

The host must *read* the works of Meher Baba, he says. "He was more than a mystic. He was an avatar. Do you know what an avatar is? Forget all the others, forget the rest, read him. He is out of print except for two books that were reprinted in 1998. In there you'll learn where to get his other books. There's only a few places in the world—one in South Carolina, Los Angeles, and one in Australia."

The host breaks in to say that she probably has his books.

"Meher Baba? You can't!" the man says. "They were last published twenty years ago."

"I have an old Big Sur house," she manages to get in. "People have given me their old libraries. There are so many things I haven't read—"

In his story the seeking is paramount. The host can't *know* Meher Baba. She has to search. All the air will go out of searching in just a few years. One or two clicks will find Meher Baba's biography, sayings, books, films, devotees. The internet makes a shipwreck of pilgrimage. You can just sit at home like some digital squirrel piling up gurus and "wisdom ways," all of which tell you not to be so acquisitive, so worldly.

"Well," says the man, interrupting the host, "if I'm telling you, then it's time to read Meher Baba." He says Meher Baba's name— "compassionate father"—was given to him by his followers. Meher Baba considered himself an "avatar," a God in human form like Rama, Krishna, Buddha, Muhammad, or Christ. "I am the same Ancient One come again into your midst," he told his disciples. Meher Baba was from India, he says.

The host's aunt is going to India. She wants her aunt to see the Taj Mahal.

"*Forget the Taj Mahal!*" he says so loudly that his judgment fills the room. Meher Baba is buried 160 miles east of Mumbai in Meherabad. Her aunt *must* go there. He hasn't been there, but one day he will make the pilgrimage.

This man talking about Meher Baba is the usual way we think of seekers—as somebody "way out" at the fringe of the continent. But seekers are all around us. This is a book about seekers, about Americans seeking their Eden, their Promised Land, their utopia out on the horizon, which, by definition, is ever receding before us. When Thomas Jefferson committed the new nation to the "pursuit of happiness," he set up the primary occupation of every American.

In this book we follow a few of these pursuits:

* A young man shepherding the Shakers through their twilight years. The end of all but one of the Shaker villages is not as usually portrayed—a dour shuffling to the end of their days. It is, true to its beginnings, a devotion.

* A group of adventuring nineteenth-century landscape painters looking for God and for signs of the future greatness of their new nation in New Hampshire's White Mountains. Tourists today rushing up the Mount Washington Auto Road were set on their course by these pioneers of seeing.

* A doctor who achieves the American Dream by changing the boundaries and ruling himself and his family in, crossing over and crossing back, rewriting the definition of race.

* Forty thousand Africans newly freed from slavery taking possession of the forty acres and a mule that were granted by one Civil War general and one secretary of war—only to have their land taken from them within months by another general and a new president.

* Veterans home from World War II, having grown up in the Great Depression, ready at last to start their lives where everything is new in the suburbs. The spindly trees grow up; the children grow up and turn against them. A collision between peace and war, the American Dream and protest, children and parents.

* The Pilgrims and the Wampanoags sitting down to a harvest feast, which would be spun into the Thanksgiving story, a fable that blinds us to the ingratitude and wars lying behind our holiday and our country's founding.

This is but a small gathering of Americans, all on the road to find out, all united by their longing and devotion. "All history is the history of longing," says historian Jackson Lears, and in each era this longing gives form and force to our lives.

SEEKING GOD

The Believers at Twilight

I. "An Honest Seeker"

The summer that Bud Thompson met the Shaker sisters he was young and they were old. They had reached the country of old age and would be old for a very long time. They would come to be celebrated for being survivors, the last of their faith. They were photographed, recorded, and venerated for their age so much that it seemed like the sisters had been born as grandmothers in long nineteenth-century dresses and bonnets. The sisters in their youth seemed like an impossibility. Old age became a mask, the way certain people are frozen with us in time—Einstein with his crazy white hair, W. H. Auden with his mud-cracked face, or Washington and Lincoln.

There were then, in the mid-1950s, fourteen Shaker sisters living at Canterbury in New Hampshire. The last brother had died in 1939. There had always been more Shaker women than men, all the way back to 1747, when the United Society of Believers in Christ's Second Appearing was founded in England and later brought to America by Mother Ann Lee. Their enemies had named them Shakers or "Shaking Quakers" for their ecstatic worship, for trembling and throwing themselves about and speaking in tongues. The days of trances and testifying, of "singing, dancing, shaking, shouting, leaping," of nighttime worship so raucous it could be heard for two miles—those days were more than a century gone. They were no longer a threatening, radical religion. The Shakers Bud met were a quiet, pious, dedicated lot, their lives shaped by thousands of days of work and devotion into a work of art itself. The Canterbury sisters were living in the twilight of the Shaker utopia.

Life had portrayed Canterbury Shaker Village in 1949 as a waiting room for death, a few breaths shy of the next funeral. The black-and-white photos showed spare rooms with chairs hanging by pegs, the sisters looking dour in their long dresses and bonnets. The last page ended with the title "The Death of a Sect" and a big photo of a tombstone that said "Shakers." No doubt, they were dead. A reader would have no idea of their daily joy, their sense of humor, their patience and kindness. No. The entire article said: Dead end.

Bud was thirty-three years old, a big strapping guy with a broad smile and lively blue eyes. He was a traveling troubadour knocking around the West, booked into schools by an agent back east. Before that, at age sixteen, he was a singing cowboy with his own radio show, fifteen minutes a week on WMEX in Boston. He may have been the only teenaged singing cowboy from Rhode Island—and not even western Rhode Island—in the whole curious history of singing cowboys. After that, for a short time, he had a lady cowboy partner. They were billed as Babs and Bud.

He visited the three remaining Shaker villages at Canterbury, Sabbathday Lake, Maine, and Hancock, Massachusetts. At their peak in the mid-nineteenth century, there had been nineteen major Shaker communities and perhaps as many as six thousand Shakers. Bud was looking for new folk songs, but all the other local folk songs had been picked clean. Alan Lomax and other "songcatchers" were recording folk, blues, and jazz musicians in the field. Bud's booking agent told him about the Shakers. They had written or adopted some ten thousand songs. The songs weren't written, the Shakers said; they were received. This was the first Bud had heard of the Shakers.

He liked the three communities, but his Canterbury visit changed his life and the lives of the Shaker sisters. Walking around the village, he ran into Sister Lillian Phelps, and they got to talking quite a while about music. Lillian had studied music in school before she came to

Canterbury at age sixteen. Lillian was very sick when she arrived. She had tuberculosis; her parents thought she would die. The sisters nursed her back to health. She decided to stay and seldom mentioned her illness, saying she had come for a summer vacation and fell in love with Canterbury. She loved to say that her vacation had lasted seventy years. Lillian played the organ—it had been bought with her in mind. She played every Sunday for the sisters and she gave music lessons. She was so moved by their meeting that she offered to play for Bud.

"They had this lovely Hook & Hastings organ" in the chapel, Bud recalled. Lillian played "Méditation" from *Thaïs*—"did a beautiful job"—and two or three other pieces. Then Lillian, who had "a little bit of teasing way about her," said, "'Now wait, Bud. We talked. We played a few things for you, and now we're expecting you to do something for us.'

"I said, 'I don't have my guitar. I don't have any music.'

"'Now, you're not getting away with anything,'" Lillian said. "She was full of fun. She was a serious and smart lady, but she also had that kind of light. She had a beautiful personality.

"She lifts up the piano seat and she pulls out some schmaltzy thing like 'The Bells of St. Mary,' I think it was. So she played the accompaniment as I sang. I think we became almost instantaneous friends."

Bud returned with his father, who sang in church and was a choir director. He had a comic routine where he'd deliver "Old Mother Hubbard" like a thundering, fire-and-brimstone preacher. The sisters loved it. They didn't know when they'd laughed so hard.

"We had a wonderful afternoon, and when we got done, Lillian and Sister Aida Elam said, 'You know, Bud, we love you. We've got to get together more often. Can we do this again sometime?'"

Music had led Bud his whole life. Music led him to the Shakers and to his two wives. His first wife, Harriett, was an organist and choir director at a church, and his second, Nancy, was a soloist at another church. He fell in love with her when he heard her sing. His life was shaped by music.

Bud left to go sing out west, driving by himself from Hurley to Verona to Sarcoxie in Missouri, to Claremore and Nowata in Oklahoma, to West Mineral to Weir and Scammon in Kansas, to Carl Junction in Missouri, to Galena in Kansas, to Carthage, Alba, and Diamond, back in Missouri, singing some days at 9:00 a.m., 12:45 p.m., and 3:00 p.m., week after week, in small-town schools on a route that also took him to Iowa and Nebraska. But each Monday he'd get letters from Sister Lillian or Sister Bertha Lindsay. He had that to look forward to, a letter or two waiting for him in Rolla, Kansas (population 464), Hurley, Missouri (population 117), and all the other spots on the map where, at the end of the day, he knew no one. Bud had given them his schedule before he left and the sisters pulled maps out of the drawers to follow his journey. He saved their letters in a big photo album.

This is the kind of devotion that happens in first love, with teens writing letters that cross town, the country, the seas. But this was the romance of an aging, celibate Christian order and a young man who sang cowboy songs and folk ballads.

They continued to write to him when he returned home to Massachusetts. Bud visited often, helping out by pruning apple trees in the orchard, painting buildings, and giving tours in the summer. Lillian wrote to him:

> My Dear, Dear Bud,
> . . . You know, whenever I find your generous "tithe," it is difficult to keep back the tears. Your sincerity, and loyal devotion to the ideals of our Shaker faith, touches me deeply, and I silently breathe a prayer of gratitude to our heavenly Father, for this bond of Christian love and understanding which is growing stronger between us and our Thompson friends. . . .
> We are having wonderful weather, and I long to be out of doors all day. . . . I walked up the road after supper, last night, and

the beauty of the hills, and tall maples, was overpowering. I thought how much you would have enjoyed it. There was such a feeling of peace and security that came over me, I wanted to share it with the whole world. . . .

Love to you all,

Your sister,

Lillian

She had a tender concern for him. "Now Buddie," Lillian wrote in another letter, "take a wise sister's advice and don't *go too fast*. You are only human, and I do want you to live as long as I do." Sister Bertha wrote him also. "It's almost impossible to keep up with thanks for all you do," she said.

The sisters were at loose ends; they missed their brethren. With the death of their last brother they had lost a powerful dynamic. They believed that God was male and female, that men and women, each working in their own sphere, were equal. And they were short of labor. The sisters could no longer run their farm. For that they had to rely on hired hands. They turned to fancy work, to sewing and selling baked goods. If the Shakers' work, whatever they were doing, was participating in God's creation, what happened when their work no longer sustained a self-reliant community, when they gave up farming and the making of chairs, oval boxes, brooms, medicinal herbs, and packaged seeds? As their work narrowed, the Shakers' world was diminished.

Bud even won the measured approval of Eldress Emma B. King, whose stern manner had left her to be called, out of her hearing, Emma *Be* King. She was in charge of the hardest decisions of their declining years, including closing other villages and the religion itself to new converts. As they closed buildings and villages, she had to weigh many requests by those looking to carry off a piece of Shaker heritage. The sisters were often asked to sell their furniture, tools, music, and historical documents.

Eldress Emma wrote to Bud, delivering her verdict: "I believe you are trying to do good in the world and are sincere in your efforts so it is a pleasure to encourage an honest seeker after truth and a high standard of living." Implied in her judgment were the others she had sent away, or maybe, in a Christian way, hosted, fed, and sent away. But the sisters loved Bud from the first.

"He hung the moon in their eyes," said June Sprigg, who spent two summers at Canterbury during her college years and later returned. She went on to a distinguished career as a Shaker museum curator and the author of many books about the Shakers. "He did so much for them, because that's Bud. They absolutely adored him. They sort of saw him as a son. I think he could do no wrong in their eyes. He was just utterly devoted to them."

They asked Bud to come work for them. He had no idea that he'd be there for the next thirty-one years.

∽

Eldress Emma was right: Bud was a seeker, but one with a touch of Barnum. He was a showman and a salesman, and that mix would come to their rescue.

He was a high-school dropout who sought out teachers his whole life. He lacked a year of math and a year of a foreign language, so he sat and watched his classmates graduate in 1941. Within months there was a war on. He volunteered for the Merchant Marine.

His education never ended; he was determined in everything he did. He had become a singing cowboy on a bet. He'd picked up his friend's guitar and plunked away on it. His friends said: You're pretty good; you should be on the radio. Maybe I'll try that, said Bud. Oh, b.s., they said. They bet twenty-five dollars that he couldn't do it in six months. Bud went and auditioned at radio stations. If he says he'll do something, he does it. His older sister Margaretta helped him get material, looking up old West stories to tell about Wild Bill Hickok and the rest. (She had given him his nickname, calling him "my little baby bud" when she couldn't pronounce brother. His given name is Charles.) She booked him into gigs all around Boston. He had no singing training. Later, he studied to be an opera singer with Alexander Kipnis, regarded as one of the world's greatest bass singers, at the Metropolitan Opera in New York.

He had also thought he might like to join the circus. He met a high-wire walker who used to practice on a low wire in a gym. He helped Bud set up a low wire for himself so he could try it. But when Bud was fifteen or sixteen he was in his father's office in the city when a parade came through. His dad's office was on the fifth floor. Bud thought he'd just walk out on the ledge and get a good look at the parade. Standing there on the ledge he discovered that he didn't like heights at all. "I was never so damn scared in my life. I decided the hell with that," he said. The circus lost a recruit. "I hate heights even to this day. That was really the wrong choice, and it didn't take me long to find that one out."

He had to learn about things firsthand. "I was curious about everything. I still have my ear to the ground," he told me a week before his ninety-seventh birthday. At the same time, a colleague said, "Bud never looks back. He has a hundred ideas." It's difficult to keep a running tally. He planted a lilac arboretum with three hundred varieties, set up an institute to study utopias and another to study the paranormal. The New Hampshire Society for the Study of Psychical Research would invite a guest, hear him out, and over coffee give the presentation a good skeptical thrashing. The sisters attended. They were open. They knew that the spirit life was present and that the departed were with them. Sometimes they saw angels.

Bud was a seeker, but never a convert. He knew the Shakers, visited the Amish, was friendly with a Hindu swami, and was inspired by a Pequot Indian sachem. He admired preachers who had built huge followings. He liked anyone walking the righteous path, but he disdained extremists. He believed in a "higher power."

"I've had a guiding power, a guiding spirit," Bud said at lunch one day with his wife, Nancy, and his son Darryl.

"We're a religious family," said Darryl, who was one of the last children to grow up at Canterbury and is an avid Shaker scholar. "We feel that God has led us. I mean that humbly—that God has opened doors for us."

"So many things have dropped in just at the time I needed them. The right things came. I have to believe it's more than just luck," said Bud.

∽

The sisters welcomed everyone who found their way to their hill in Canterbury, a small town fourteen miles north of the state capital. (Just the name Canterbury implies pilgrimage.) Canterbury Shaker Village was twenty-nine buildings on a hill, mostly wooden, mostly painted white, lined up neatly with rows of old maples and white fences. It was pleasing, the buildings—large and small houses and barns—set out as a child might, lacking the usual configuration of buildings facing a street or a parking lot. In this setting, visitors found harmony, serenity, simplicity, grace, a solace for the soul. That's what they told the sisters over and over. They found virtue; they found belief, even if they, themselves, were not believers.

The sisters were sought out by seekers: by a woman named Peace Pilgrim who had walked across the country twenty-five times preaching peace (and still had the strength, when invited to dinner, to denounce the sisters' love of Cool Whip); by a Santee Sioux, Red Dawn, who "adopted" them in a ceremony; and by all sorts of spiritual sightseers, a few claiming to be prophets or angels or the bearers of a new religion. Since their earliest days, the Shakers had invited the World's People— as non-Shakers were called—to witness their worship services.

In their last decades, they didn't play the part of the pious Shakers. When they first met Bud, they performed "some schmaltzy song," not, as you might expect, a Shaker hymn. They were believers; they did sing Shaker songs, but they confused and surprised people with their sense of humor and TV watching—Sister Gertrude Soule loved watching *Wall Street Week* best of all because Louis Rukeyser was "so handsome." Sister Ethel Hudson liked watching *General Hospital* until "all the nurses started getting pregnant."

The sisters were smart and lively; a few were cranky, but they, too, were admirable. They were funny in the way they trafficked in worldly goods, with odd adoptions of twentieth-century American materialism like an electric carving knife and a big KitchenAid mixer. Some appliances were just a continuation of the Shaker quest for efficiency, and others seemed off-key, like the way non-natives speak a foreign language, often emphasizing the wrong words.

One photo captures it: Sisters Marguerite Frost and Edith Clark in their long dresses and bonnets are standing with saxophones. They loved music, yes, but the saxophone? It's funny, joyful, unorthodox. The two sisters are smiling at the camera. In a stricter era, no musical instruments were allowed. The rules had eased and the Canterbury sisters had several musical ensembles, including a ten-piece harmonica band called "Tenuvus."

They took a serious delight in the World's People, and they charmed many of their visitors. Maybe their visitors couldn't define it just then—and the sisters never preached—but there was something that moved them about these last Shakers. They said they were the most lovely, honest, direct, welcoming people they'd ever met.

There were, by the 1950s, more buildings than sisters. Eldress Emma was faced with closing Canterbury and sending the remaining sisters to a nursing home. At the village's peak in the 1840s, 260 Shakers lived and worked in more than one hundred dwelling houses, barns, workshops, farm buildings, and nine water-powered mills running on an extensive system of seven ponds and dams. On three thousand acres, they grew apples and peaches, made maple syrup and candy, and ran a productive dairy in New Hampshire's largest barn. They sewed distinctive women's cloaks; made wooden pails, boxes, and baskets; sold packaged seeds; ran a print shop; and made many improvements in how work was done, including patenting a steam-powered washing machine. They ground their own flour, wove their own cloth, tanned and cured leather for boots and shoes, made bricks, candles, butter and cheese, hoes, scythes, wagons and their wheels, brass clocks, and copper tea kettles. Their neighbors may have been puzzled by, or hostile to, their faith, but they respected their prosperity. "This establishment is immensely rich," Nathaniel Hawthorne reported after an 1831 visit. "On the whole, they lead a good and comfortable life." (He even considered joining, but he was put off by "their ridiculous ceremonies.") As their population shrank, they took down buildings and sold land until they had about two dozen buildings and hundreds of acres in hayfields, orchards, and woods.

The Shakers had a wild beginning. In England, the woman who was to become Mother Ann Lee joined a small group of renegade Quakers who regarded themselves as the only true believers. They would charge into churches to disrupt services. They repeatedly spent time in jail. One of her group had a roadside vision of America as a shining tree on which "every leaf . . . shone with such brightness, as made it appear like a burning torch, representing the church of Christ." They left for America. Mother Ann, with seven others, arrived in 1774 on the eve of the Revolution. Being English, they were suspected of being spies and spent more time in jail.

There was a millennial fever in the land. Ann Lee and her followers joined a chaotic churn of breakaway religious beliefs: New Lights, Free Will Baptists, all sorts of believers in the coming of the millennium and a reunion with Christ. Crowds came to see Ann during her five months in jail and later at the small Shaker farm near Albany, New York. Some believed she could see their sins, and that she had the light of God. Her singing, they reported, "could instantly fill the assembly with inexpressible joy and rejoicing." She began to win converts.

Mother Ann's Shakers, the United Society of Believers in Christ's Second Appearing, are not the Shakers we know. They are not the pious, well-ordered, "hands to work, hearts to God" industrious makers of spare, beautiful chairs, songs, and art. Not the wizard-creators of the circular saw, flat broom, clothespins, and wrinkle-proof cloth. The Believers are spirit-drunk; they speak in tongues, screech, whirl, tremble, shake, eat dirt, race back and forth in frenzy for hours, dance and shout, sing ethereal, wordless songs, make so much joyful noise unto the Lord that their church services are "a perfect bedlam." Time and again observers report worship that is far from the quiet rooms of tasteful Shaker objects we know. They were crazy, ecstatic, mad, even. They rejected all scripture except the Bible. They sought to live by finding proof of God's presence.

Ann and her small band traveled through Massachusetts and Connecticut seeking converts. They targeted towns where other breakaway faiths were seeking a path forward, converting many Freewill Baptists. They were attacked, clubbed, caned, whipped, thrown from bridges, and kidnapped. Several times Ann was taken from her bed and physically examined to see if she was a woman or a witch. In Harvard, Massachusetts, a mob stormed a house, carrying off two Shaker brothers who they tied to a tree and whipped. In Petersham, Ann was dragged downstairs "feet first" and thrown into a sleigh like "the dead carcass of a beast," fracturing her skull, an injury that may have led to her untimely death a year later at age forty-eight. Other towns put their revulsion on record as Henniker, New Hampshire, did at Town Meeting in 1789: "Voted that we will not have any dealings with the 'Shakering Quakers' living in town."

After Ann's early death, Brother Joe Meacham "gathered" the church "into order," establishing the leadership of elders, eldresses, deacons, deaconesses, and trustees. Meacham set up communal villages and decreed that they should be an orderly heaven on earth. Much of what was allowed in Ann's day was put aside. He formalized the three key tenets of Shaker belief: celibacy, communal life, and confessing your sins. Order was now the face of Shakerism.

But the spirit life broke out once more in a new generation, fifty-three years after Mother Ann's death. Angels visited the different Shaker villages, each time by first physically seizing children.

"It came as a thief in the night," reported Elder Abraham Perkins of

Enfield, New Hampshire. "It was first manifested in the little girls of ten and twelve years, while in the religious service. It seemed to be a power that exercised them in dancing, shaking and whirling. Some would remain unconscious for hours while conversing with unseen friends and singing new and beautiful songs. . . . Some of the little boys were thrown violently to the floor, and it was with difficulty that they were removed.

"Their visions became more and more convincing. The visionists were taken into the mansions of the saints and shown the glories of the heavenly worlds. At other times they would be conducted to the abodes of the wicked, the sight of which would seem unbearable. With tears they would beg to be removed from such terrible scenes."

The spirits moved on to adults, moved on to appearing as Indians, foreigners, enslaved Blacks, George Washington, and Mother Ann, moved on to dictating books, art, and song. The "visionists" delivered warnings and prophecy, prescribing new rules. Most visionists were in a trance for "only a few hours," but several were entranced for two and three days. The longest recorded trance was six days. At Canterbury, the spirit messages filled 450 manuscript pages in just six months.

"Indeed, the heavens seemed to have opened and the treasures of the celestial Kingdom were given as from the hands of angels," wrote Canterbury Elder Henry J. Blinn. "All hailed the dawning of this new day with gladness, and pleasant anticipations were the order of the religious service. The minds of the audience were also changed into that of astonishment."

The angels were not among them for a night or two, but for many years, spreading among the different Shaker communities, speaking in strange tongues, singing haunting songs, and guiding hands to create surprising, radiant art. For fourteen days, "a mighty angel" dictated, through a visionist, the "voice of the living God" for a book that ran 450 pages, *A Holy, Sacred and Divine Roll and Book*. A few years into this revival the Shakers called the New Era or Mother Ann's Work, the spirits directed the Shakers to create holy feast grounds and to take up holy names for their villages. Canterbury was Holy Ground, and nearby Enfield was Chosen Vale, and so the map of America was populated with the holy: Holy Land, Holy Mount, Holy Grove, Lovely Vineyard, Pleasant Garden, City of Love, City of Peace, Vale of Peace, Wisdom's Valley, Wisdom's Paradise.

The boundaries of earth and heaven touched and sparked. Angels were talking to the Believers, and soon, they prayed, the angels would walk the world, announcing themselves to the World's People. It was as if a once-placid river was raging, jumping the banks, flooding the land. The angels were near.

Quieter times returned. The ten years of Mother Ann's Work ended by 1847. But the spirits never really left.

"Now as to spiritual power, it is as real to us as the electrical energy of the universe," Canterbury Sister Marguerite Frost told an audience in 1960 at a series of lectures arranged by Bud. "By it, believers have written books, worked out interesting dances, received songs, drawn beautiful designs, and healed sickness.

"Spirit life, we believe, is all about us. It is everywhere, as is God, in him whom we live and move and have our being. Those who were once in visible condition, as we are now, are with us, influencing us to a greater or lesser degree as we seek their help. Our physical experience on this earth is life's elementary school, a preparation for the life of the spirit, which will be endless. All life is progressive, ever leading to new light and truth. Year by year, even on this earth, we believe spirit life will become more manifest.

"The dangers and tragedies of life need not happen. If we know that we are surrounded by spiritual influences, there are no accidents in Christ, the Shakers taught. As the morning sun dispels the shadows of the night, so the glory of God, the spirit life, is yet to remove the darkness of earth life."

The Shakers had long ago given up their distinctive dancing at worship meeting. They no longer shook and trembled, but they still "lived life on the boundary between this world and the next," said

Shaker scholar Priscilla J. Brewer. Another monastic, Thomas Merton, knew that boundary. Merton had visited the silent, closed Kentucky Shaker village not far from his own monastery. He wrote, "The peculiar grace of a Shaker chair is due to the fact that it was made by someone capable of believing that an angel might come and sit on it."

~

The Shaker sisters Bud knew stood at another boundary: they were almost all orphans.

When the Shakers were "gathered into order," founding their villages, entire families had converted and joined. Later in the nineteenth century, the villages became a refuge for widows and orphans. The Shakers added to their population by taking in orphans, but at a bad rate of return. They would care for dozens of children, and one or two might stay and sign the covenant at age twenty-one. By 1840, a long population decline had already set in.

The sisters' lives as Shakers began with a death in the family. They were dropped off by relatives or passed from hand to hand until they arrived under the Shakers' care. "I was taken into the Shaker home at five years of age on September 26, 1878. My father was failing in health and went looking for care for his children. My mother died at my birth," said Eldress Emma B. King. She was one of three surviving children in her family. Her older sister was already at Canterbury. Her father, "by trade a carpenter," had consumption. "The doctor said he must work out of doors, so he drove the horse cars for a year and then took his bed" and died. Addressing an audience in 1960, she speaks precisely, each phrase chiseled, her inflection even, her recorded voice a little thin, nasally, old-time New England. This is an aged voice vaulting across the years. Emma was born in 1873; she was eighty-seven.

The sisters weren't taking any more small children, and because Emma was "delicate in health they felt it would be a good deal of care." Her father, "unwilling to be defeated," brought her to Canterbury anyway to spend a few days visiting her sister. The sisters agreed to "try her."

"One time I was reported as not going to live. The sisters were very good to me, cared for me. I was taken out of school and spent a whole summer out in the sunshine as much as possible, and I recovered sufficiently to make sure of life for a while." She would "keep a teaching practice" at the Shakers' school for "about twenty-three terms"—"I was not able for the heavier work of the home"—and she moved up in the church leadership.

The Shakers treated children with the "utmost tender affection," Emma said. She recalled a childhood lesson. She "felt very sorry" for doing something "that was not right" and asked for "forgiveness" from Eldress Dorothy Durgin. "She took me by the hand and led me to the west window. It was in February and a most glorious sunset was off, and she pointed up the excellence and the majesty of God's presence in the world and that it was the duty of us all to honor that glory and majesty, and to copy in our lives the best and most perfect things that God represented. It was a very soulful occasion and left an indelible impression upon me, and I think it had quite an influence upon my life."

The Shaker villages were populated with these stories, which were invisible until the sisters and brothers consented to talk about themselves. One of the sisters who Bud knew best, Eldress Bertha Lindsay, arrived at Canterbury in 1905 on a stagecoach with the mail. Her parents had died within a month of each other. She had an older sister who was headed west to get married. She left Bertha in Canterbury. Bertha was almost eight years old.

"I will never forget my first day," she said. "My sister, Mae, left me here with tears streaming down my face. I did not know what to expect." She threw herself down in the dirt road, kicking and crying. "Then Sister Helena Sarle came along and said, 'Don't cry, little girl. I'll be your sister.' And true to what she said, she was a sister to me as long as she lived."

The next Sunday was Apple Blossom Sunday in Canterbury Village.

"Everyone was singing and marching and they swept me right along to the apple orchards on the Shaker farm where they gave praise and thanks to God. Birds were singing, the trees were filled with apple blossoms. It was beautiful. I began feeling the love and warmth of the people here. This has been my home ever since."

Eldress Bertha was renowned for her cooking. She worked long hours, up at four-thirty cooking and cleaning up until she took a break in the afternoon at two. Then she returned to make the evening meal. In summer, some years, she was cooking for twenty-five hired hands in front of a big wood-burning cookstove with two ovens big enough to cook a ten- or fifteen-pound roast and four pies at once (until that was replaced with an electric stove in 1940). For a weekend she would prepare an amazing twenty-six pies. In her stories, Shaker life is one large, inviting kitchen filled with pies, roasts, and, in season, the smells of pickle making. She did all this calmly, with joy; she never let on that she got tired.

"They just loved her," said June Sprigg, who has fond memories of Bertha. "They made her feel part of being at home, and when she raised a girl, she passed it forward."

"That's the best thing the Shakers ever did, was raise all those kids who fell through the cracks. That's better than any round barn or oval box," Sprigg said, noting two triumphs of Shaker design. "That's what they did. They provided homes for kids, and most of them left over time. It was a very generous thing to do. I'm a stepmother and I think about Bertha raising these girls and then having them leave and not come back and not live there." And as Bertha got older there was no one there for her. Her best friend, Lillian, who was like a "mother figure," died seventeen years before her. "Bertha didn't have a Bertha. She was very brave. There's a lot of courage in that."

∽

Alberta MacMillan Kirkpatrick was the last girl raised by the Canterbury sisters. The Shakers were no longer taking children by the 1920s, but Sister Marguerite Frost (who had spoken of spirit life) desperately wanted to raise a little girl. Each year before Christmas, the sisters were asked to list three gifts they might like so the eldresses could pick one and have it under the tree. Sister Marguerite made her list: *1. A little girl 2. A little girl 3. A little girl.*

They got the message. Alberta needed a home; they agreed to take her. She had lived in six different foster families; she had been neglected and abused. "I was very upset," Alberta recalled. "I had considered suicide." Alberta was eleven, just a year older than Sister Marguerite was when she came to Canterbury after her mother's death. She had walked uphill from the train depot in a snowstorm, getting blisters on her feet. "The sisters seemed to me like angels, they were so kind," Marguerite recalled. "I thought I'd never be good enough to be a sister."

The day Alberta arrived she was scared. Living with foster families was grim. Some families made her watch as they ate dessert. No foster child was good enough for dessert. "I can remember sitting in the parlor over there at the office and they had called Marguerite and I saw her come running from the Dwelling House. And it was wintertime, December 29, so she had her heavy wool cape on, was holding her bonnet. I could see the cape fly in the wind. That's how fast she was running down, and I thought to myself how disappointed she's going to be when she gets here and sees me. She's not going to like me."

Alberta was "cringing," hiding at the back of a sofa. "When she got into the door she fell right down on her knees and put her arms out to me and said, 'Darling I thought you would never arrive.' It was very emotional for both of us. . . . She was the first person who hugged me since my mother died when I was six. And she just was so affectionate to me and made so much of me and told me what a lovely little girl I was."

Nobody will ever hit you, Marguerite told her. "You're going to be my little girl." She made me into "somebody entirely different than the little girl that arrived here. There wasn't anything I wouldn't have done for that woman. I adored her."

One night Marguerite came in and didn't want to disturb her. The next night Alberta left her this note:

> Please give me a kiss to-night even if you think I look to nice
> to be kissed.
> Lovingly Alberta

Alberta grew up, and when she was eighteen she wanted to go out into the world, go to dances and movies and date boys. "It was a very sad thing leaving Sister Marguerite. She had always called me Birdie—she never called me by my first name. And she said, 'Birdie, it's your time now to fly.... There's no life here for you,' she said. 'If you stayed, we're all getting older. Your life would be taking care of older sisters and sick people. And I don't think that's what a young girl should face.'"

Alberta visited Marguerite every year for her birthday, which was near Mother's Day, so it was like a combination of both, she said. Marguerite and the other sisters "made me the person I am if I am at all good. I just can't imagine the person I would have been."

Canterbury Shaker Village was an orphan's utopia, a place striving for perfection, run by women from homes broken by hardship and death. They understood children; they were patient with visitors. The sisters had adopted Bud and he had adopted them.

II. "A Blanket of Blessing"

Late in life they faced losing their home again. Bud didn't want to see the remaining sisters shipped off to a nursing home. Eldress Emma was prepared to close the village; she was selling furniture. (She'd knock on the door to tell a sister to empty out the desk she was using. It was sold.) It'd be a shame to lose this, Bud thought, as he walked through empty buildings. "If these people go, we've lost everything." It made Bud sad. Canterbury sometimes felt like the beach in winter "when everything is boarded up and the people are gone," he said. "I have often stood here on a summer night and thought, if only we could turn back the clock and see what this place was like with all the people here. They were a world within a world once upon a time."

Bud thought Canterbury could become a museum, but he envisioned something more than they could imagine. Several of the sisters—Lillian, Bertha, and Marguerite—thought that, yes, they could display furniture and old clothing and so forth in one of their buildings. Visitors would like that. But Bud meant that the entire village, and the old orchards and hayfields and ponds, would be an "open air museum." They were puzzled. You can't put all those old chairs and hymnals outside on tables, they said. And, of course, that's not what he meant.

Bud had to show them; he had to sell them on his idea, and here's where they were fortunate that this "honest seeker" was also a salesman who knew how to put on a good show. He had learned from the best. His father, Alexander, was one of the two top sales executives for the A. Nash Clothing Company. He had worked his way up selling custom suits door-to-door. He'd knock on a stranger's door, convince him that he needed a new suit, take his measurements, and in a few weeks the stranger was wearing a suit that would turn the heads of his neighbors.

This may be where Bud picked up his habit of telling corny jokes, real groaners. Salesmen don't care if you don't laugh; the joke has worked if they have your attention. A traveling salesman's jokes could be earthy, a bit blue. When Bud's jokes alluded to something a little racy, Sister Bertha would caution him, saying gently, "Oh, Buddy," so that they were both winking at a joke he'd never tell.

He took his allies, Sisters Lillian, Bertha, and Marguerite, on field trips to successful outdoor museums. They went to Old Sturbridge Village in Massachusetts and Shelburne Museum in Vermont. Canterbury could be like those museums, collections of old buildings and tools with guides who were sometimes in costume, except that those museums had been assembled with buildings from many places and the guides were dressed up to portray the past. Canterbury was in place, and there were even a few living Shakers who could play themselves—but there would be no dress up. The Shaker costume was a religious habit. They wouldn't have their villages turned into a masquerade.

The sisters liked Bud's idea, and they eventually won over several other sisters, but they had to convince Eldress Emma and then have all the sisters agree. Lillian, the first Shaker Bud had met, was his advisor. She had a keen understanding of strategy. She probably could have succeeded in corporate boardrooms.

"Don't call everyone to a meeting in a room and present the idea to them as a group," she told Bud. "If one person speaks against it, the others will be reluctant to speak for it. Instead, present the idea to each sister individually. Discuss it with each, ask for the thoughts of each, and refine your ideas to incorporate as many of their suggestions as possible. Build consensus and a community of support. Then, carried on this tide of unanimity, you can present the idea to Eldress Emma." Bud made the rounds, campaigning for a museum.

Lillian told him when to present his idea to Emma at her office. "After you leave, I will arrange for [Sister] Aida to go to Eldress Emma's office and express her full support for the project. Then I will contrive to accidentally-on-purpose meet Eldress Emma on the walkway as she crosses over to the Dwelling House, and I will say, 'Eldress Emma, did you hear about Bud's wonderful idea?' and will express my enthusiasm for the project. Still later in the day I'll arrange for [Sister] Ida to visit Eldress Emma and give her full backing for the project."

Emma was surrounded. She agreed to the museum—temporarily—until the village was sold to a religious or charitable group and the last sisters were in a nursing home. In some ways the change to a museum was a new "gathering into order," the next generation of the Shakers' idea. Bud set up a museum in the Meetinghouse and they opened a few buildings. He had been collecting cast-off Shaker furniture and tools for years. Visitors began arriving; it was more like they had dropped in on their neighbors. Bertha and later Gertrude welcomed them—they were "guests never tourists"—and sent them out with Bud. The sisters offered the hospitality of a home, not an organized museum. "I'd finish taking a few people around, and a few more, and a few more, and I'd be worn out," Bud recalled. "Then I'd get a call from Lillian and she'd say, 'Oh, Bud, there's the most lovely people here.'" And around Bud would go again. The first year as a museum in 1960, five hundred guests dropped in for a visit. The young museum was amateur in the best sense of the definition: "something done for the love of it."

~

When the World's People began to arrive, what did they want? They came first a few dozen at a time, then fifty to a hundred on a summer's day, and then forty and seventy thousand in a season. Some were surprised to be greeted by a living Shaker. Mostly it was all they could do to keep from saying, *but we thought you were all dead.*

Bertha and Gertrude looked like grandmothers from another century. They had beautiful smiles, kind faces. Wearing close-fitting caps, they seemed not archaic, but ageless. They wanted to see the best in everyone. They let people relax a little into their best selves. "We're giving them a feeling they've never experienced. They feel the love and the influence when they step here into this village," said Gertrude. "And this particular lady came into the front hall, and she said, 'When I came up the road and saw the white buildings, it was much like a blanket of blessing that went around me.'

"Some of them come in tears and they want to take our hands. And they just love it," she said.

People saw what they wanted to see in the sisters: living antiques; models of serenity and sanctity in a time of Mutually Assured Destruction. Believers. Constancy. At different times, people discovered the Shakers they were looking for—in the 1960s, the commune that worked or the pacifists who had resisted the Civil War draft; in the 1970s, a feminist society. They were a communal island in a sea of individualists, kind in a world that valued competition and rough strife. In their hillside quiet, they seemed like a throwback. They were formal. They lived their belief, lived not to speak ill of others, to do good work aiming for perfection, but accepting that they'd fall short. They were with Christ; they were sure in their faith even as the Shaker life was fading. They were still Believers, and that's what they wished people would see.

The museum began to grow up. Eldress Emma B. King died in 1966. With Marguerite and Bertha in charge, the museum would be permanent. It was formally incorporated in 1969. Bud was no longer the only tour guide, but he trained everyone. It was his tour.

On Bud's tours he told visitors that the Shakers were an amazing, hard-working people. Look at how much these people had done, at their inventions and workmanship. He always focused on the positive. Sure, they had problems; everyone has problems. The Shakers were unique, benevolent, and charitable. We can learn from them and try to be better people. "What is Canterbury Shaker Village?" asked one newspaper advertisement. "Bud Thompson's Spirited Tours."

At each stop on the tour, in each building, Bud had a showpiece, something that would grab the attention of even reluctant visitors like the husbands trailing along at the back of the group. He'd show them the Shakers' cleverness—the tilting feet on chairs, a long-handled broom to sweep the ceilings of barns, the clothes-drying racks that rolled out of the wall. Then they woke up and came forward to talk to Bud as they walked along. "By the time I got done the guy would be all turned on. It was rare that I couldn't turn him on," he said. A tour guide had to be enthusiastic, Bud said. If you're not excited, the public won't be either.

This was a show he also took on the road, lecturing about "the Friendly Shakers," as the promotional flyer said. ("DO YOU KNOW that the Shakers . . . were the FIRST people in this country to raise, package, and sell Garden Seeds and Medicinal Herbs . . . were the ONLY successful communal organization in America.") Sometimes he would bring the sisters with him. "It was a love fest," recalled June Sprigg.

If the tour guides got too far from "Bud's tour," as it was known, they might get the "cookie talk." Bud would say, let's you and me go have a cookie. He'd tell them that there were too many facts in their talks and not enough heart. He understood that people wanted to connect with the Shakers. He wanted visitors to be inspired. A tour should be like a good play or any performance that gives you a larger view of your life. Otherwise, why go?

"People come here to get away from the world and to escape their problems, and we want to leave them with a good feeling. You need to touch the heart more," Bud said in his cookie talk, Renee Fox recalled. Renee had started at Canterbury with a summer job in the gift shop more than thirty years ago and was a tour guide before becoming the museum's archivist. The tour guides were free to give the tour as they wished, but all the tour stops were set and the guides were frequently overheard by other guides and staff. Bud "definitely kept an eye on us," she said.

Bud didn't talk about the radical, early days of Mother Ann and the later spirit fever. He avoided "anything that was messy." Guides were frequently asked about the Shakers' celibacy. "So, if someone asked, 'Well, did the Shakers ever run away and get married?' And if you said, 'Well, yes, they did,' and then came up with some examples, I mean, that wasn't part of Bud's tour," said Renee. "If someone asked him one of those difficult questions, he would say 'I'm interested that you're interested in that question.'" He didn't answer; he put it back on the visitor. "Bud didn't want us to go in that direction," said Renee. "Bertha used to say how she was witnessing for the Shakers who had gone before. Bud was witnessing to the existence of this community and the things they had done, rescuing them from what could be oblivion."

"He saw in the Shakers this wonderful potential of the human spirit and their generosity and this marvelous vision of human society," said another former tour guide, Brad Fletcher. "It was very idealistic and he just wanted people to get imbued with that. And I actually think they did. I mean, people going to the village and on the tour . . . reacted in ways that this was far more than just visiting a historical site. There was something authentically spiritual about the place and that, I have to say, is really, I think, Bud's gift."

Brad was a tour guide in the summers while he was in college. He went off to the Peace Corps and returned as a guide while getting his master's in American history. He wrote his thesis about Canterbury before becoming a prep-school teacher. He loved being there and admires Bud, but on his return his view of the Shakers had changed. He was reading the latest scholarship. "I came to believe that there was a real disconnect between Shakerism at its height and Shakerism by the time of the last Shakers that we knew. . . . I think this is really hard when you're dealing with the last survivors and the true believers of a group realizing that they are trying to shape a legacy." The nineteenth-century Shakers were a rule-bound, doctrinal church, he said. Bud didn't see it that way. He was concerned that Brad had "soured on them," which he hadn't.

The Canterbury sisters had left the young museum a puzzle: How do you tell the story of nearly two hundred years of devotion? How do you make a museum about faith? It may be almost impossible. In Europe, rivers of people, a *roman touriste*, flood the great cathedrals, looking, taking selfies, talking so loudly that the few faithful trying to pray are almost swept away. In some cathedrals I've heard announcements reminding visitors that this grand *object d'art* is a house of worship. Brad was confronting that puzzle, trying to show the different seasons of Shaker belief.

Bud was telling the Shaker story as Lillian and Bertha knew it—a looser, more liberal Shakerism than its nineteenth-century heyday, when rules upon rules were issued and revised in 1821, 1841, 1845, and 1860, dictating rising and retiring times, a five-foot minimum distance between brothers and sisters in the Meetinghouse (which they were to enter "in the fear of God walking on their toes"), and banning, at different times, many secular books, "perfumery," whispering and winking between brothers and sisters, pets, coffee, tea, and pork. In Bertha's last years she said the Shakers "have no creed: we simply believe in living by the teachings of Christ as he taught them. It's the Golden Rule."

Bud's tours weren't an academic symposium. He can be impatient with anything he sees as criticizing the Shakers. One day he said to me, "So there's the guy Darryl told me about, just coming out with a new book. And I think he made the criticism that I was too idealistic. Well, all I knew was what I knew. I knew them and lived with them—he didn't. By and large I never worked for people that to me were more what I think Christianity ought to be—not what it *is*, but what it ought to be."

Bud ended his evening candlelight tours by taking out his guitar and singing at the Meetinghouse. For a time the village had all the guides sing at the end of their tour. It was awkward and, for some tone-deaf guides, painful. In a Meetinghouse lit by candles, Bud led a sing-along of "Simple Gifts" and followed that by singing a Shaker song he had discovered, which he called "Brother Ricardo's Song." In the late 1950s, Bud had visited Brother Ricardo Belden at Hancock Shaker Village in Massachusetts. Ricardo, the last brother at Hancock, was a versatile mechanic, repairing clocks, especially old ones with wooden works. He was eighty-nine and sang with a strong voice. Bud loved to hear him sing. During one visit, Ricardo sang "a spirit song" that the Shakers had received, probably during the era of Mother Ann's Work. Bud drove away committing it to memory. It's a keening lament, with words in no known language.

> Mee   lo may nee oh   Ah nee lee mo oh
> Ah   nee lee mo oh   Ah nee lee mo oh

It feels at once ancient and familiar, a haunting melody that reaches deep inside you.

Bud then told a story from Robert Louis Stevenson's boyhood. Stevenson was very sick; he spent months in bed looking out at the streets of Edinburg watching "people coming, people going. Everybody busy. The sounds of horses' hooves and wagon wheels rumbling over the cobblestone streets. . . . He said that as the afternoon wore on and twilight came, from out of the night came an insignificant little man. Insignificant even by daylight, let alone by night. He was the old lamplighter of Edinburg, whose job it was to light the lamps along the street. Insignificant little man. But he said, one thing impressed me about him: wherever this man stopped to light his lamp he left a beautiful, glowing lamp.

"It kind of reminds a little of the Shaker story. Because when the Shaker people started out, they were considered an insignificant little group. People didn't pay much attention to them. Some of the more sophisticated people described them as just a candle in the sun. Not very important. They went about living their life quietly. There was a period when people looked and said, 'Oh they're dying out. It's too bad. They were good people, kind people. Too bad.' And then students and scholars took a second look and they jumped back in utter amazement at what this little group of people had achieved. Insignificant, perhaps, but like the old lamplighter of Edinburgh, what a lovely light. Their membership started decreasing. They're almost gone. But you know what? There's never been a time that the light has shone brighter. There's never been a time when more people have come to listen to their words and find out who they are. People are amazed at what this group has done. I think they let us see that people don't have to live by greed and aggression. . . ."

He closed the evening by leading everyone in singing "Edelweiss," because he had taken the sisters to see the *Sound of Music* and all the way home they had sung "that lovely melody."

"It was romantic," said Renee, recalling Brother Ricardo's song rolling out into the night. It was stirring. She doesn't remember anything else about that tour, but she remembers that. A romantic evening, the starlight, the crickets, the mist coming off the hills, moving through the orchard, and Bud singing. People didn't forget it. Maybe they couldn't have told you anything about the Shakers' travails, or explain what they believed about Christ's second coming, but they knew the Shakers were special people.

~

Mother Ann had prophesied that when they were reduced to a handful, the Shaker ideal would return. And indeed there was a revival, not with newly committed Shakers, but with the World's People eagerly taking an interest in everything Shaker. There were lavish books, museum exhibits, documentaries. Shaker furniture brought astounding prices. Celebrities bid serious money to collect simplicity and grace.

The Shakers, by the 1970s, were like a national pet. They were seen as a living museum of old-time American values of hard work. They had stayed down on the farm. Their celibacy was seen as eccentric. Their furniture was hymned on high. To the World's People in the late twentieth century, the Shaker religion was a work of art. It was a still life—a few chairs hanging on pegs, twin stairways meeting in an empty room as polished as a jewel box, a small stack of oval boxes, a Shaker sister in her bonnet and dress. It was an American edition of a Vermeer painting, a few objects, daylight slanting in the window, stillness, silence, and grace.

They had gone from being attacked and ridiculed in the nineteenth century to being regarded as eccentrics of no matter in the early twentieth century to being venerated as artistic exemplars coming down from the mount to deliver Shaker chairs and boxes and cupboards and pegs, songs, and spirit paintings. They were like a devout Bauhaus.

"We're an endangered species, so people like us," said Gertrude.

The Shakers became a product with Shaker chair kits, all manner of "authentic" Shaker touches like Shaker kitchen-cabinet pulls, and "Shaker polo" shirts from Land's End. Shaker dance was advertised as the "aerobics of yesteryear."

The Shakers were upstaged by their good work, their beautiful furniture and villages, their smart inventions. They were prisoners of their furniture. "I almost expect to be remembered as a chair or a table," said Eldress Mildred.

By dying off, the Shakers had fulfilled the definition of utopia—the good place that is no place.

~

In the end, when they were down to seven women, they knew the Shaker life was over. Only two sisters lived in the fifty-six rooms of the large Dwelling House, Sisters Alice Howland and Ethel Hudson, with her six-toed cat, Buster. One sister and a longtime resident who had never signed the covenant lived in a couple of rooms in another large house. The other three sisters—Lillian, Bertha, and Gertrude—lived across the road in the Trustees' Office and checked up on the others at least once a day by calling on the old crank telephone and sometimes visiting in person. They had sold much of their Shaker furniture. The sitting room in the Trustees' Office was furnished with upholstered chairs and a couch, a TV, knickknacks, and a caged parakeet. The room was painted a bright, bubble-gum pink. They no longer dined together at the long tables in the Dwelling House. They were too few to pray in the Meetinghouse. Bud drove them to church in a nearby city. At Christmas they decorated an artificial tree.

"We are now just a group of older people trying to care for each other, maintain our homes, doing what good we can and salvage what good we can from Shaker history of the past," Eldresses Frances Hall and Emma B. King wrote to a reverend in Ohio. But in a public statement of her belief, Emma wrote: "The material homes may fail but the Shaker experiment is no failure. . . . God has permitted us in our humble way to do much good. The principles, the light and truth will live on forever." And at the only other surviving village, Sabbathday Lake, Eldress Mildred said, "It is good and therefore of God and no good is ever a failure."

Carrying a belief across generations is an achievement, a Herculean effort to maintain clarity of purpose and practice amid the muddle of human emotions. The question isn't why they died off, but how did they hold it together for so long?

"Everything authentically Christian is rooted in the fact that I wish to be part, or connected to God. And I see that I'm not. And therefore this produces a kind of fire, a kind of yearning, and that is the core of everything," said philosopher Jacob Needleman. A community united in faith and work kept the fire going. The Shakers were longing for God.

Eldress Lillian Phelps died in 1973, Eldress Gertrude Soule in 1988, Eldress Bertha Lindsay in 1990, and the last, Sister Ethel Hudson, in 1992. For the first time in two hundred years, since they were "gathered into order" at Canterbury, the Believers were gone. A few Shakers did remain at Sabbathday Lake, but that part of America that was the City of Peace, the Chosen Vale, Holy Ground, that part of America was no more.

Bud was asked to sing at their funerals, but he couldn't do it. He had trouble even talking about losing his sisters decades later. He left Canterbury to found the Mount Kearsage Indian Museum. He had been collecting baskets and canoes and pottery and clothing his whole life. He put aside every penny, wearing the same suit for years, driving an old rattletrap car with holes in the floor, just to keep collecting. He'd been set on this path in the second grade when Chief Silverstar came to talk to his class. At age sixty-eight, Bud wasn't too old for new ventures. People around Bud tried to talk him out of it. He was near retirement age, after all, and established historical museums were struggling to hold the public's interest. Dartmouth wanted his collection, but Bud refused. He put everything he had into the museum and it took hold. He was celebrated for his tenacity and vision. At age ninety-seven, Bud was awarded an honorary high-school degree.

"What we need are more Bud Thompsons out in the world, more people that are willing to sacrifice their time and attention to serve other people," said Ken Burns, who met Bud when he was making his second documentary, which was on the Shakers. Part of it was filmed at Canterbury, "one of the most beautiful places in America," said Burns. "It's like standing on the rim of the Grand Canyon." Having grown up studying American Indians, Burns admired the "love and care" he saw in Bud's Indian museum. Bud "had a clear obsession with trying to remember who these people were and to remember it with a kind of sensitivity and spirituality."

He felt indebted to Bud and counted him as a mentor. "I am who I am in large part because of the people on whose shoulders I've stood over the many years, and I've stood on Bud's shoulders for a long time. So if you know who I am, it has a lot to do with him," Burns said. "I think that we're all fortunate to have somebody like Bud who's there to remind us what a life well-lived could be."

～

On the night she died, Bertha wrote her last letter on earth. It was to Bud. It was found at her bedside the next morning. In a shaky hand that fell crookedly across the page, she wrote:

> Please dear Bud take time to care for yourself better. . . . You are so dear to me. I wish it possible for me to take away all your worries, but I have you lovingly in the hands of our Father to ask [him to] walk with you, guide you & bless you. . . . With all my love, Bertha.

What were you worried about? I asked him one afternoon. "About the village and the end of it. I didn't want to see that happen. And the worry that I would lose them. In fact, it was Darryl and I that spread Bertha's ashes after she died. It was her request that we do that. She loved Darryl and she loved me."

～

On a raw, windy day in March, I was early to meet some people at Canterbury, so I walked uphill to the front of the Meetinghouse and stood there looking out at the rolling fields below. The Meetinghouse faces a small common lined with old maples, a perfect outdoor room that feels secure and rich. Elder Henry J. Blinn saw to the planting of the oldest of the big maples in 1859 and 1860. Each was named for the child who took care of the tree. Bertha was the last one who could remember the child's name that went with each ancient maple. I felt good standing there; I felt reassured, happy. The place hums; it smiles back at you. It's what the ancient Celts called a thin place, where heaven and earth are close, a holy place.

Two hundred years of devotion changes souls, changes the soul of a place. Two hundred years of devotion changed this hilltop in New England. But there's also a lot of hardship in the Shakers' story. Hiding in there is an unreckoned ratio of suffering to contentment. What does it take to create a few acres of peace? And would we know peace—true peace, not just the walled-off opposite of no war, no hate—but peace: Would we know it if we see it? It's here on this New Hampshire hill. It feels powerful, deep, resonant. *No good is ever a failure.* That's what I think about as I drive down the hill, round the corner, and Holy Ground disappears from view.

"WE ARE STILL IN EDEN"

Awe on the American Plan

I. Like a Turkey Swallowing Corn

On a summer's day, the road up Mount Washington has the hall-mark upheaval of a tourist attraction. Wave after wave of cars and motorcycles move with the percolating hurry of a ferry crossing. We watch the light glinting off the cars miles away up the mountain, little flecks of glass in the granite and the green. It's mesmerizing. If you didn't know better, you might mistake this for an evacuation up the mountain.

I've come north to the mountains with a friend who is an artist, James Aponovich, at the time New Hampshire's artist laureate, in search of the scenes that appear in the great landscape paintings of the nineteenth century. The base of the auto road may seem to be an odd place to begin a pastoral quest, but the impulse that sends more than thirty thousand cars and trucks hurtling up the mountain each year began with artists back in the 1820s. Today's tourists may not know it, but they've come in search of an Eden created by a legion of nineteenth-century landscape painters. Their paintings taught Americans how to look at the wilderness. Americans were eager for the lesson, and, with guidebook in hand telling them where to see the views in the famous paintings, they followed the artists. Their art created a market for the views, filled hotels with tourists, and laid the bounds for state and national parks and forests.

This mix of restlessness amid grandeur has long marked the visitors' chase. Thomas Starr King, the go-getter Unitarian minister and author of the most popular nineteenth-century guide to the White Mountains, lectured his readers in a minister's tone to slow down: "A large proportion of the summer travelers in New Hampshire bolt the scenery, as a man, driven by work, bolts his dinner at a restaurant," wrote Starr King in 1859. "Sometimes, indeed, where railroads will allow ... they will gobble some of the superb views between two trains, with as little consciousness of any flavor or artistic relish, as a turkey has in swallowing corn. . . . There is no *smack* in their seeing."

Except for the mention of the railroad, Starr King could have been with us on this summer day. Is there "smack" in our seeing?

The road up Mount Washington was begun early, in 1854, at a time when the country lacked good roads and bridges. There was plenty that needed doing elsewhere. Building a road up the highest mountain in the Northeast would not have made any list of necessary public works for a young country. The carriage road was one of those nineteenth-century engineering projects that seemed to be propelled by a force as powerful as a religious calling and a biological drive. No one questioned the wisdom of building a road up a mountain known as a cauldron of ferocious weather. And like other works of its era, the road is handmade, built by men working ten- to twelve-hour days, drilling blasting holes by hand in the granite, sleeping in shanties and tents, carrying supplies eight miles from the nearest railroad station by horse, by oxen, or on their backs. After three years of construction, with the road at the halfway point, the company ran out of money. A second company was founded two years later to finish the road.

"America's oldest tourist attraction" opened in 1861. Tourists rode in wagons and coaches to a small summit hotel. The road was forecast to be the beginning of a great resort. There was talk of extending the seven-and-a-half-mile-long carriage road along a ridge to the summits of Mounts Clay, Jefferson, Adams, and Madison. "The rivalry of hotels on tops of the mountains will be as sharp as it is at Newport, Saratoga or Niagara," said the *New York Times*. But after only eight years, the carriage road fell out of fashion when the cog railway to the summit opened in 1869 on the west side of Mount Washington. The short train ride beat the all-day journey on the road. Building railroads everywhere was another signature American obsession. (Had they built a canal up the mountain, they would have hit the nineteenth-century transportation trifecta.) By the late 1800s, the summit had two hotels, the carriage road and the railroad, an observatory, a telegraph, and a daily newspaper. The only things missing, really, were a mill, a church, and a school. The summit was like an amusement park with a great view, "the second greatest show on earth," P. T. Barnum reportedly said about the view or the cog railway—and even if he didn't say it, staking the claim was right in the spirit of the age, pure Barnum.

The arrival of the automobile revived the road. The first automobile made it to the summit in 1899—a steam Locomobile driven by F. O. Stanley, later known for the Stanley Steamer.

The auto road is a family business. It's owned by four families. In the New England manner it seems more like a public trust. The five-dollar toll for a car and driver did not increase for sixty years, holding steady from 1911 into the 1970s. The iconic bumper sticker—*This Car Climbed Mt. Washington*—first appeared in the 1930s, a badge of honor in an era when radiators overheated on the way up and brakes overheated on the way down. No one knows how the bumper stickers got started, but they are all over the world. The road's general manager, Howie Wemyss, mails out replacement bumper stickers to Europe and the Mideast. Foreign tourists are fans of the road. They travel a loop from Boston to Mount Washington to Acadia National Park on the Maine coast.

As the general manager, Wemyss (pronounced weemz) is the road's curator and protector. He has worked at the road since the 1970s. He is the author of something seen by every visitor starting out on the road. He wrote the warning sign:

ATTENTION
THE MT. WASHINGTON AUTO ROAD IS A STEEP,
NARROW, MOUNTAIN ROAD WITHOUT GUARDRAILS.
IF YOU HAVE A FEAR OF HEIGHTS, YOU MAY NOT
APPRECIATE THIS DRIVING EXPERIENCE.
GUIDED TOURS ARE AVAILABLE.

People do "freak out," he said.

"It's pretty constant that every year we will drive down from the summit about two dozen cars—motorcycles, too. People that have somehow managed to get themselves to the summit and then they think of that drive back down, and a particular stretch of road where on the way up they're on the inside, and now they know they're going to have to be on the outside. And they can't do it."

The distress calls are not from older drivers, who are from an era of rougher roads and rougher cars. "The twenty- and thirty-somethings coming out of the city are just blown away," he said.

Mostly what concerns Wemyss is that people are in too much of a hurry. They race up his road to see the view up top, which on most days isn't there. He is sad that people don't take the time to enjoy the road itself—"the auto road experience" as he says. On some days you can see more than a hundred miles, see five states, Canada, and the ocean. On other days the view may be eight feet. Wemyss sounded like a Zen master counseling pilgrims to appreciate Mount Fuji in the clouds—however you find it, the mountain you see that day is the mountain. Or, as he says, "So frequently the view is not there. And the experience is always there.

"What we're trying to do is to get people to think of it as more than a place to go for a good view. In reality, the environment up there is so different than the rest of New England that it's worth the drive just to see what's up there on the ground. It's the same as driving into northern Labrador. You're driving to the Arctic Circle—it's going to take you half an hour to get there. It's fascinating." Every one thousand feet of elevation is equivalent to moving about one hundred fifty miles north. But visitors are hemmed in by the heritage of scenic tourism; they are looking for the one view—the snapshot—and they hurry on. In view-seeking they reduce the "experience" to a picture.

"How long do people spend on the summit?" I asked.

"When we last surveyed it, I was disappointed, I should say. We found that they spent about forty-five minutes." He was crestfallen. He had a host's pride in the mountain.

"That's a lot for an American," I said.

"Well, apparently it is," Wemyss said. "I would have thought that people would have been more interested in all of the various things that are up there. Spend more time up there. But you know they've got to move on. They've got things to check off their list today."

They have tried to slow down visitors and get them to look *at* the mountain. They offer a one-hour stay in the mornings, but some people ask, "Do we have to stay an hour?" Admittedly, on most days the summit of Mount Washington is not a picnic spot. The observatory up top boasts of the "world's worst weather."

"We tried a three-hour tour the last couple of years. You go up and actually get out and walk around a little bit. It's flopping. Nobody cares," he said, dejected.

~

The first pilgrims who made their way through the notches, the mountain passes that open the White Mountains to the world, faced far rougher travel, but they, too, were quick to criticize others for their haste. It was an era of slow journeys by foot, horse, and canal boat. It took Timothy Dwight, president of Yale, who wrote about his travels, fifteen days to go from New Haven to the White Mountains in 1797. Forty-two years later, Henry David Thoreau was seven days traveling by rowboat, foot, and stagecoach from Concord, Massachusetts, to Crawford Notch.

In the early nineteenth century, the turnpike through Crawford

Notch was so rough that wheeled carts couldn't be used. It was so steep that ropes had to be used to pull up a horse that was harnessed to two long poles dragging on the ground. The cargo sat on a board lashed between the dragging sticks. This was like forgetting about the invention of the wheel. Going downhill through the notch, they had to tie a rope around the horse's neck to keep it from falling. Most travelers walked, and most freight was moved in the winter on sleds. Before 1825, the two inns then near the notch were twelve miles apart, a serious distance, presenting a challenge to travelers to arrive at one before nightfall.

One of the first artists to paint the White Mountains, Thomas Cole, arrived in Crawford Notch six or seven days after leaving Concord, New Hampshire, ninety miles away. Today that ninety miles, almost all of it by an interstate highway, can be covered in an hour and a half, but our speed undermines our arrival, as if everything we see is still blurred.

The artists who introduced this northern wilderness to America were walkers. The great landscape paintings were born at a walker's pace. They spent days approaching the mountains. They saw Mount Chocorua far away and saw it slowly grow, day by day. They came through Franconia Notch riding atop a stage and felt the curving wall of Mount Lafayette pushing toward them. If they were to hike up a mountain like Chocorua, they'd first walk a half dozen miles to get to the mountain and then start their way up.

Cole, traveling with a friend by wagon and foot, had to contend with washed-out roads and bridges. They crossed the Swift and Saco Rivers several times, once in a canoe that "came close to upsetting" and other times by "means of fallen trees and rocks and I may add firm nerves, for it required no little courage to venture on such precarious bridges with a rapid stream rushing beneath," he wrote in his diary.

They walked through Crawford Notch just two years after a great rockslide had killed the Willey family in 1826, a disaster that fascinated the public. The site would become one of America's first tourist attractions. "We walked among the rocks and felt as though we were but worms, insignificant and feeble. . . . We looked up at the pinnacle above and measured ourselves and found ourselves as nothing," Cole wrote. In the paintings he made after his trip, the notch is a forbidding wilderness. Facing nature we're insignificant, and that is what makes us significant. That's one of principles of the sublime: we are humbled by God's power; we find our place in the world. The sublime was a specific experience, a twining of wonder and fear brought on by wilderness, towering waterfalls, thunder, and tempests. Awe is the word that is used: worship and reverence in the presence of the sacred. "We now entered the Notch and felt awe struck as we passed between the bare and rifted mountains that rose on either side thousands of feet above," said Cole.

The mountain wilderness was "a fitting place to speak of God," he said. In America we can still see "the undefiled works" of "God, the creator." The "prophets of old" found inspiration in the "solitudes of nature," and that inspiration is there for us to claim. "It was on Mount Horeb that Elijah witnessed the mighty wind, the earthquake and the fire and heard the 'still small voice'—that voice is *yet* heard among the mountains!"

This land with "its beauty, its magnificence, its sublimity" is every American's "birthright," but they don't live up to their inheritance, said Cole, who was born in England and lived there until age seventeen. "They wander 'loose about'; they nothing see, . . . short lived, short sighted." Beautiful places are being destroyed—"the ravages of the ax are daily increasing"—"in this age, when a meager utilitarianism seems ready to absorb every feeling and sentiment." But "Nature has spread for us a rich and delightful banquet. Shall we turn from it? We are still in Eden; the wall that shuts us out of the garden is our own ignorance and folly."

To the first white settlers, the White Mountains were not Eden. The mountains were avoided. They were a "daunting terrible" wilderness "full of rocky hills" and "clothed with infinite thick woods." To

Europeans since the time of Christ, mountains were "Warts, Wens, Blisters, Imposthumes." Travelers in the alpine passes of Switzerland asked to be blindfolded to avoid the terrors of looking at the peaks—it might drive them mad. The Alps were home to witches and many species of dragons. Mountains were "Nature's Shames and Ills," a libel against God's perfection. God had created the earth six thousand years ago on the third day of Genesis and there it sat, unchanged. The earth itself, it was widely believed, had no history. Within fifty years in the eighteenth century, all this changed. Geologists, Romantic poets, and artists discovered a living, dynamic earth. It was "one of the most profound revolutions in thought that has ever occurred," says scholar Marjorie Hope Nicolson. In America, Cole was a leader in this revolution in seeing.

Cole's paintings made him famous. He was the premier American landscape painter in the first half of the nineteenth century, and a teacher and friend to other painters who were portraying the wonders of the Hudson River and the Catskills. Aspiring to do more than just paint scenes, he pursued a "higher style of landscape," one with moral lessons, like his two paintings of the Garden of Eden in which the mountain is modeled on Mount Chocorua, and sweeping allegories like the five paintings showing the rise and fall of civilization. Cole died early of pneumonia, at age forty-eight, at the height of his fame. "I think every American is bound to prove his love of country by admiring Cole," wrote diarist Philip Hone.

America was Eden. God was present. A view of eternity awaited in the mountains. Scores of artists, backcountry adventurers, and tourists would echo Cole.

Climbing Mount Carrigain with friends, the Rev. Julius Ward reveled in "the sense of utter separation from humanity, the sense of entire lostness in the wilderness, the sense of complete abandonment of the soul to Nature," as he wrote for the *Boston Sunday Herald* in

1890. He stepped away from his companions to "feel this aloneness in all its intensity" and "to measure my heart-beats by the rhythm of the life of the mountains."

"There is something about one's thoughts on these desolate peaks that can not be spoken, just as there is something that one never tells about his religious life," said the Reverend Ward.

In the mountains, Benjamin Brown French, clerk of the US House of Representatives and a New Hampshire native, was moved to sing. He was ecstatic. He loved good drink, "glorious chowder," and fishing. ("We fished nearly to sunset & caught 130 trout.") At one inn he and his friends "duly disposed of" a pitcher of eggnog and "sang and danced & enjoyed ourselves mightily." (Did they have more fun back then?) But approaching Crawford Notch by horse and wagon, he was reverential:

"Sunday, June 29 [1845] . . . The scene about us became awfully grand & majestic. It was a temple not made with hands in which all the aspirations of a man's soul must necessarily rise to the God who formed it. I felt that the day & the place were sacred. Though no great singer, I could not resist bursting out with 'Old Hundred' & Henry joined me, and I declare that I never felt more solemn or more in the immediate presence of the God who made me, than when, among those everlasting & eternal hills."

One visitor excelled in this Junior John Muir League of Moralizing: Thomas Starr King, the Unitarian minister who wrote the era's most popular guidebook to the mountains, *The White Hills*.

There's a sermon on every page in *The White Hills*, a moral lesson in almost every paragraph. At 403 pages, this is an exhaustive and exhausting guide, a mountain of prose to lay before the mountains. Every view comes with a preachment to throw off your triviality. Starr King is like a Moses of tourism who never ascends the mountain to receive the Ten Commandments, but instead lectures his flock on the right way to look at Mount Sinai.

He tells the reader what to see and at what time: At about four on a summer's afternoon, view the Great Stone Face, the famous profile of the Old Man in the Mountains, from the little lake below. Best of all if there are thunder clouds behind the stone face (in which case I'd suggest leaving the lake). He also judges the Great Stone Face to be melancholic and having a weak mouth, as though suffering from bad teeth. It's the most heartfelt description of the profile that I've ever read. You get a sense that Starr King would like to cheer up the Old Man.

His guidebook not only sets out specific views, but lectures his readers on the proper way to look, to travel. When he scolds tourists for their haste, his scorn goes to the heart of how they live, holiday or not. "The difficulty is, that in rushing so fast as many of us do through the mountains, the mountains do not have time to come to us," he writes. Who has earned their scenic view? Who's really in the Church of Nature for the right reasons, to pray to God, and not just for the social after? The mountains are God or God's house and we are not worthy, not paying attention.

And not any mountain view will do. The view must be "framed" correctly, must be more than land; it must have the qualities of a landscape painting. The mountain must be at the "proper distance" so there is atmosphere, color, and light. "There must be meadow, river, and greater distance from the hills, so that they can be seen through large intervening depths of air. Going close to a great mountain is like going close to a powerfully painted picture; you see only the roughnesses, the blotches of paint, the coarsely contrasted hues, which at the proper distance alone are grouped into grandeur and mellowed into beauty." It's not enough to see Mount Washington; one must see it as it has been seen in the better paintings.

Tourists wanted to see the landscape as art. Many carried a Claude Glass to make the landscape more painterly. Named for the French landscape painter Claude Lorrain, the glass was a tinted, convex mirror that looked like a makeup compact. A viewer stood with his back to the scene and looked at the mirror to give the scene a "mellow tinge" and the glow of Lorrain's paintings. Thoreau sometimes carried a homemade Claude Glass in his travels around Concord.

Seeing is Starr King's real subject. Slow down and look at the mountain for as long as possible. See it on a misty day and on a "day sacred to clouds." Be there at sunset and sunrise. He has the dedication of plein-air painters. Get outside. Look and look again, sketch, return and look again, sketch and return, and maybe the place opens to you. Maybe it "hums" as the twentieth-century installation artist Robert Irwin said. Driving across the Mojave, "it's all just flat desert," mile after mile, said Irwin, but in an instant "it takes on an almost magical quality. It just suddenly stands up and hums, it becomes so beautiful, incredibly, the presence is *so* strong. Then twenty minutes later it will simply stop. And I began wondering why."

Irwin went to great lengths to rejuvenate his vision, closeting himself in an anechoic chamber, where no light or sound entered for six to eight hours. Once he got out, the world had shifted; everything seemed to be saturated in color and energy. "Nothing is wholly static, that color itself emanates a kind of energy. You noted each individual leaf, each individual tree. You picked up things which you normally blocked out."

Similar encounters occurred in the White Mountains. In this "daunting terrible" wilderness, the world shifted for a generation of artists. Their paintings are a story of first sight, insight, and learning to see again.

"The general beauty of the world is a perpetual revelation, and if we are impervious to its appeal and charm, a large district of our nature is curtained off from the Creator," Starr King wrote in *The White Hills*. "As soon, therefore, as we become educated to see, and just in proportion to our skill in seeing, we get joy." A few years later, preaching from the pulpit, he told his congregation, "I believe that if, on every Sunday morning before going to church, we could be lifted to a mountain-peak and see a horizon line of six hundred miles . . . we should feel that we live amid the play of Infinite thought; and the devout spirit would be stimulated so potently that our hearts would naturally mount in praise and prayer."

The White Hills went through ten editions in more than twenty-five years, but Starr King didn't stay around to live on his success, to tour the lyceum circuit imploring his listeners to slow down. He hurried on. Just a few months after his book was published, Starr King moved to San Francisco to take charge of a church. He continued his energetic travels. He was smitten by Yosemite, comparing it to Beethoven's Ninth Symphony. He'd seen a lot of granite in New Hampshire, but that paled before Yosemite. "Great is granite, and the Yo-Semite is its prophet!" he said. He wrote home to a friend: burn my book:

> Dear Randolph,
>
> I have . . . descended into the jaws of the Yo-Semite. Poor White Mountains Notch! Its nose is broken. If you can find any copies of King's book on the New Hampshire ant-hills, I advise you, as a friend of the author, to buy up the remaining edition and make a bonfire of these in the park. . . .

The booster, the landscape cheerleader, had found a grander stage. Starr King's allegiance had migrated, just as the great landscape painters would, heading west to paint Yellowstone and so many other shrines to the sublime that would become national parks.

He lectured tirelessly in California, campaigning for Lincoln and for the state to stay in the union. He opposed slavery and raised money for the United States Sanitary Commission's work to help sick and wounded Union soldiers.

Starr King lived in California only four years, becoming the state's "man for all seasons," says one historian. He died young at age thirty-nine, from diphtheria. In the US Capitol's National Hall of Statuary, where each state is allowed two statues to represent its best, Starr King stood for California until he was replaced by Ronald Reagan in 2009. His statue was moved to the California state capitol. There is another Starr King statue in San Francisco's Golden Gate Park, and there are schools, churches, streets, a park, and, most appropriately for this prophet of granite, two mountains named for him, one in Yosemite and the other in the White Mountains.

~

The great nineteenth-century landscape paintings were encounters with a little holy terror. They implied that God was near. They were about a vast land, about wonder that bled off the canvas. The huge mountains suggested mountains without end. They suggested that greatness without end awaited the young nation.

The paintings were exhibited in Boston and New York. They were news; they were an advertisement of a great find, a scenic Gold Rush. The tourists followed by the trainload, filling the big wooden arks of the hotels. They stayed for weeks. They came back to the same hotel year after year. The hotels expanded, burned, and were rebuilt ever larger. The arrival of each new railroad line spawned more hotels and additions, a wing here or there, forming H-shaped, T-shaped, L-shaped buildings, farmhouses multiplied many times: window, window, window, dormer, dormer. Longer and longer runs of clapboards unrolling like yards of linen. White, boxy buildings, crisp as a starched shirt. The hotels advertised the lengths of their piazzas. Imagine yourself lingering to take in the view, promenading after dinner. (They are piazzas, *not* porches.)

More artists followed the tourists. A half dozen of the grander hotels had artists in residence. Other artists, like Benjamin Champney, had set up studios nearby. Champney was lured to North Conway with the promise of reduced room and board if he'd put the town's name on his sketches. It worked. There were soon forty artists in the neighborhood painting. They painted the scenes that tourists saw from their hotels or nearby, walking, or on a carriage ride. They painted the same scenes over and over and they painted them in a size ready to go home: ten by sixteen inches, postcard size, a few two by three feet. The foreground is bucolic, settled, husbanded, sometimes with cattle. The distant mountains are big, recognizable in profile, and not menacing. They are dignified, familiar, presiding. Sometimes there's a storm coming or going, but blue skies prevail. They are *nice* paintings, easy paintings to live with. They are paintings with parlor manners. They would hang on the wall in the front parlor or hall, politely in the background until you chose to look at them. The great views were domesticated. Awe was downsized to prettiness.

The landscape went from being a testament to a souvenir; visitors went from witnesses to tourists on the American plan—a room and three meals, all included. No revelation, no burning bush, just sightseeing. The artists no longer insisted *you must look at this.* They painted pretty pictures. Benjamin Champney's studio was near a big, popular hotel. Tourists could shop for the scene and the size painting they wanted to take home. There are more than a hundred paintings displayed in a photo of his studio. "If I have not accomplished anything great in art, I have at least given pleasure to the inmates of many homes," he said.

For the first artists, the White Mountains was a place awaiting their discovery, a place they would conjure. By the end of the nineteenth century, after all the paintings and guidebooks, it had all been seen. A visit to Crawford Notch or Franconia Notch was a paint-by-numbers exercise. The views and the corresponding emotions were prescribed. Look here and look here, do this and this, quote this writer and that one. Time soon for dinner, a game of cards, a stroll on the piazza.

The best of the landscape paintings are a call and response, a longing and its echo—Is God here? the painter asks, and the land answers *yes.* The paintings are a longing for arrival, a longing to feel at home in this Not Europe land; a longing to find God and God's approval, to read the Bible in the mountains, rivers, waterfalls, and valleys. Do not turn away from it, says Thomas Cole, almost as a commandment. "We are still in Eden." The modern viewer stands before the grand landscape paintings and the echo is different. *Is God here?* And the echo returns only his question.

II. In Search of "Visual Magic"

One autumn my wife and I spent a few days hiking from hut to hut in the Presidential Range of the White Mountains. The Appalachian Mountain Club runs the huts, staffed with a young "croo" who make dinner, show you to your hard bunk bed, and gather everyone after dinner to tell us, for god's sake, to "drink in advance of thirst." Sometimes they'll put on a skit trying to deliver this simple message.

You meet other hikers in the huts, and after dinner there's a lot of time to sit around and talk. That year we kept running into recently divorced men in their thirties. They were confused and adrift. "She said, 'I've grown beyond you,'" one told us, looking at us as if to say, Have you ever heard of such a thing? "I don't know why I'm walking," he said, and then treated us to a flood of talk so earnest it was bound to ruin any quest, scare off any evanescent moment. He was looking for a sign, a way forward, an epiphany, a pardon perhaps. In the hut's logbook, the bewildered seeker left a long quote from the *Tao Te Ching*, all about flexibility and rigidity, being like a flower not a rock, and so on. (Other hikers left comments that were, unknowingly, right in the tradition of the sublime. "The view is *awesome!!*" wrote one twelve-year-old boy.)

We had similar conversations with more divorced men at other huts that year. Why are you here in the mountains? they asked, as if you could dial up a transcendent moment if you had the right hiking gear and made it to the summit on a good day. Why are you walking? These hut-to-hut walkers were like the nineteenth-century tourists, like the artists, too. All of us want something from the mountains—activity, repose, renewal. We ask a lot of granite and pine, water and sky.

On the day that I stood with my artist friend, James Aponovich, watching cars and motorcycles race up Mount Washington, we were just two more guidebook-bound seekers wanting something from the mountains.

James grew up in New Hampshire, in Nashua, an old mill city on the Massachusetts border that is known today for its sprawl and malls. Though he is a native, he had seldom been north of Concord, the state capital. He described our trip to the North Country as "going to see New Hampshire." His whole adult life he has known the White Mountains as the artists had painted them. He has known Thomas Cole's mountains and John Frederick Kensett's mountains, and here, just a few hours into his visit, he was squinting at this race to the summit. James wanted to know if "visual magic was still happening."

He made a face that looked as if he were tasting a lemon. When he does this, he is in a painter's world. He's surveying, auditioning the scene for composition, color, and light. Did this place speak to him as the mountains had spoken to the earlier artists? Could he catch a moment when it leaps to life, "hums" as the Mojave had for Robert Irwin? I stepped aside, let him be, making a note to ask him later about what he saw.

I had visited Nashua with him and his wife, Beth. I had insisted on it. He didn't want to go, and once we were there, I understood why. In Nashua, as in other mill cities, the mills are like red brick dams. They rise four or five stories, close to the narrow sidewalks, casting the streets in Manhattan-like canyons of bluish shadows. The dam wall repeats, window after window, block after block. In that repetition is the story of a mill city. Day after day making shoes or cloth until your life goes by. A mill city's life is repetitive or it fails and the mills shutter.

James's family worked in the mills, his grandmother in the "shoe shops," his father in a sweatshop that made cheap luggage, "a scene like Dickens. Hell itself," said James. His mother was a clerk at an insurance company. He grew up in a cheerless home with a distant, cruel father and a mother who had such a dark outlook that she was known in the extended family as the "black hole." His grandparents were laid siege by drink and depression. His mother's father drank to a stupor, the cigarette in his mouth burning down to his lips. James would come upon his mother's mother sitting alone, crying. She'd been shipped to America from Poland at age thirteen, not speaking English. A few years later she was forced into an arranged marriage. In her wedding pictures she's angry. Her husband spent his last years in a mental hospital. James would wait outside while his mother visited, working with a learn-to-draw kit. His grandmother was a hard worker, setting aside enough on mill wages to have a duplex house built, send her daughter to secretarial school and put a son—James's uncle—through Harvard. She rented out one side of the small duplex. James's family lived with her on the other side. He shared a room with his brother.

As a boy, he found refuge in the city parks and ponds by the Salmon Brook. He knew "every muskrat hole, every inch" of the rushy recesses along the river, the park, and the ponds. He fished and swam there, and at age sixteen had his first job as a lifeguard. The park was his little bit of Eden. "My release, my way of getting away from it, and I did daily, was to go into nature where I sought solace," he said. He learned solitude; he learned about life and death. For years he walked by a fallen tree. One day it was covered with mushrooms. Life was this moment, but it was also ever-renewing. He still has a map he drew of his favorite pond. He also hung out with a neighborhood friend, drawing on boards from coal bins. As if recapitulating history, they drew animals, the cellar coal bin a Cave of Lascaux. He remembers how much he enjoyed drawing; he'd never experienced that kind of pleasure before.

He struggled in school; no one had noticed until he was in the third grade that his right eye was twenty/eighty, one quarter of normal vision. Trying to see the blackboard, he frequently had headaches and was nauseous. He had cheated on the eye tests so he wouldn't get in trouble. He dreaded parent-teacher nights; his parents would come home and beat him. At age eight he drew a picture of his father whipping him with a big whip. "He was a very violent man, very unloving and uncaring." James was also left-handed, which to his mother was a sign of the devil. She forced him be right-handed, which just scrambled his brain, leaving him even more uncertain. He began stuttering.

His father, retired from the navy, made James and his brother stand for inspection. They had to sit up straight at the table, no leaning back. They had to call him "the Boss," not Dad or Father. His father never celebrated anything; he refused to accept gifts from his sons. His mother tried her best with birthdays and Christmas. There were no books, no bedtime stories, no art in the house, no flowers—"Why buy flowers when they're just going to die?" said his mother. In later years, his parents never went to one of their son's art shows, never stood full of pride before any of their son's paintings, which are in the permanent collections of Boston's Museum of Fine Arts and the Art Institute of Chicago and about twenty museums across the country. Though I had known him for years, James had never told me any of this until our tour. He believes that you are responsible for creating your adult life. You are not fated to repeat the sins of your father. He has no patience for people who parade themselves as victims of their childhood.

The chief message of the Nashua of his childhood was to stay in your place. It was a city of immigrants, each wary of the other groups. The city was strictly sorted by parish: the Irish ruled the lower classes, grasping respectability as merchants; the Polish were next; and the French Canadians, the most numerous, were the last to arrive and thus the most despised. Main Street ran downhill from the wealthy North End—which "was like the promised land of big houses and big lawns"—toward varying degrees of poverty in the tenements of the East and West Ends, and the striving working class in the South End, where James grew up. At the high school, the kids from the North End and the South End used different entrances. "I was well aware of my standing in life. You were reminded of it every day," he said.

One day when he was fourteen years old, James and a friend were walking around the North End looking at the big Queen Anne and Shingle Style houses. A cop stopped them.

"Where are you from?" he demanded.

"The South End," they answered.

"Get outta here. You don't belong up here."

If you had seen James back then walking along the street, nearly blind in one eye, stuttering, you might have said, "You see that kid? See that Polack?"—for that is how you would have talked—"That kid is going nowhere." That's what his hometown taught him. There was no one around him saying: be an artist, follow your "bliss," live up to "your potential," and other such feel-good talk that lives in nice suburban homes.

James was depressed for a week after our visit and I was, too. Any time he returns to Nashua he gets nausea. I had expected it to be grim, but I was unprepared for the layers of oppression, each building on the next like eons of limestone pressing down, fossilizing any bit of life. It was a dark and claustrophobic childhood.

In college he studied geology first, then, after seeing a Degas or a Renoir still life with flowers and experiencing his "first aesthetic seizure," art history. He borrowed a friend's paints and brushes and began to paint. Time and again he was told that he wasn't an artist, that he "didn't have it." So he studied by himself, teaching himself perspective and composition. He took the masters of the Italian Renaissance as his teachers. He admires the freshness and discovery in their work.

His adult life is the obverse of his childhood. He and Beth take time to celebrate. They are accomplished cooks, gracious hosts, spirited, ambitious gardeners, and devoted parents to their daughter, Ana. Art brought them together. Beth is an artist who composes still lifes in pastel, oil, and pencil. Their life and their art are one. Everything they do is "about making something harmonious and beautiful from elements. Cooking. Gardening. It's not always conscious, but you find it happening," he said.

They are a close couple seen together everywhere, even if it is just the weekly trip to the town dump or the hardware store. I've joined them on sketching trips. There is a long foreground in making a painting. They go to work first by looking. You could easily miss this kind of work. It's a lot of ambling around—looking and sketching and looking some more. They quietly discuss what they're seeing with the economy of language of two longtime married people, shorthand talk that is more like thinking aloud. Coming down a hill, James stopped the car and said: "I like the thrust of the pointed balsams against the softness of the hills." Beth took a photo. He propped his sketch pad on the steering wheel, studying the scene, before sketching a series of vertical arrows with a bowed line behind suggesting a hill. He liked the darkness of the balsams against the lighter green hill. When they are working like this, they will return to the same place many times at different times of the day, take time always for a good lunch, and amble around some more, scouting out other locations. As Beth said when they were sketching a few houses, "when you draw, you feel each building."

James is known for his portraits of flowers, often against imaginary Italian landscapes. The flowers are precise and heroic, visions of a more perfect order. When he paints flowers they are idealized, larger than life, freed from the Japanese beetle that ate them. He lets them be their true selves.

If the flowers in James's portraits are aristocratic, Beth has given him a head start. The tulips in Beth's gardens seem to have an extra dimension. They are larger and more colorful than most tulips from a florist. A florist's tulips seem meek and repressed when set down near these tulips. A vase of her pink French Menton tulips has nobility. Her striped parrot tulips are ablaze. They command attention in a room. These are the tulips that star in many of James's paintings.

When they built a new house about fifteen years ago, they began the gardens years before construction. Beth planted one thousand bulbs, as well as annuals. The Aponoviches ran a garden-to-canvas operation. The season flowed from the garden through the studio. They view gardening as they do painting and sketching. "There's no difference," said James. "Gardens are a living, breathing sculpture."

The flowers on his canvases are also living and breathing, because he's painting more than just the surface. There's a depth animating these scenes. "If I am painting a peach, it's not just the soft, furry flesh outside, but the hard pit inside," he said. If he's painting an empty pot, he paints that emptiness. And he paints the air.

When a painting lives, you are aware of the air—the air has a life, he said. "You can see paintings that just look dead. They look dead at the surface; they look flat. There's nothing fluid in there. There's no movement." These paintings lack the "invisible, uniting force" of air that "goes way back into the landscape and comes forward again. It becomes the thing that transforms it from two dimensions— something you can knock your fingers on—to something that you can inhabit. Your depth of field is infinite. And through that you come back again, and go around things visually," he said, reminding me of Starr King pleading for tourists to see the mountains "through large intervening depths of air."

"You go back to the Chinese, and they said a painting is a journey where your eye wanders for thousands of miles. You have to bring the viewer through, around everything for a total understanding of the reality that's occurring," James said.

His paintings are a happy journey for many viewers. At the Currier Museum of Art in Manchester, New Hampshire, I've stood near one of his paintings—*Castello Nuovo: Still Life with Day Lilies and Watermelon*—just watching people look at his art. Many were smiling. Two women were talking about where they'd hang that painting, if they could, back home, you know, over the blue sofa. When I told James this, he smiled broadly. (Another woman has had this painting tattooed on her arm.)

"There is an unmistakable joy in the paintings of James Aponovich," said Thomas B. Parker, associate director of the Hirschl & Adler Galleries in New York City. Parker curated a show of James's art. "Few still lifes are as unabashedly positive or visionary. With their exuberant color, billowing clouds and twisting ribbons, these distinctive combinations of landscape and still life are mood-altering. Their vibrant light and almost palpable details seem to spill off the canvas. . . . These works are celebrations of the life James and his wife Elizabeth have built together with their daughter. . . . Know these paintings and you will know James Aponovich. They tell of a life well-lived—the stuff of dreams and happiness."

My friend is an escape artist, but that's probably true of every artist and writer, of anyone who shapes something out of his life. In the happy scenes of flowers and fruit, the pit is hiding, the still center is hiding, giving form to the entire show.

~

I had organized James's trip "to see New Hampshire." I had plotted a great circle route that wheeled us clockwise through the notches—Franconia, Crawford, and Pinkham. Heading for home, we stopped at Cathedral Ledge. We were visiting the sites of the great paintings as you might visit, in some churches, the Stations of the Cross. We were moving through the mountains at a very un–Starr King–like rate.

It was an odd day. My usual trip, with my wife, is an early morning beeline to a trailhead and a day of hiking in the mountains—Washington, Eisenhower, Lincoln, Lafayette, and others. We don't keep score; we do have favorites. But on this day with James, we stopped at rest stops and tourist viewpoints we'd always driven past. We were marking the bounds of where the nineteenth-century painters had worked. A few of our stops:

Echo Lake

We arrived as modern travelers, after parking. The Echo Lake parking lot took us by surprise. It was a large empty lot with a row of imposing motorhomes parked at one end, about a dozen white boxes, looking like huge refrigerators lying on their sides, pulled tightly together. In the shadow of the boxes were families at tables having breakfast. In the rest of the lot, two overweight kids, age eight or so, were riding tiny "pocket" motorbikes—fleshy blobs tottering over comically small motorcycles looping around and around. "Oh my God, circus midgets," said James. The whole scene looked like a depopulated Fellini film—a Fellini scene after budget cuts.

We walked down to the beach, where there was a strong sewage odor. The beach had been raked. A bathroom and snack stand crowded the shore. A few canoes were on the lake. At the far end we could see traffic hurtling by on Interstate 93: buses, trucks, and motorhomes racing north. In that view was the recent history of Franconia Notch.

Echo Lake was an oft-painted scene, the small oval serving as a tranquil foreground for the steep mountains of the notch. It was one of the beloved places of this "little Yosemite," along with the waterfalls and pools of the Flume Gorge and New Hampshire's symbol, the Old Man of the Mountain. The old paintings of Franconia Notch have a sweet presence; they sit in their own light and quiet. It's a small, wild world, like a wilderness in a bowl. The notch was a complete world conjured by the artists.

Thomas Cole loved Echo Lake and its close companion, Profile Lake. Standing here about 180 years earlier, before snack stands and parking lots, he was moved to rapture by this "wild mountain gorge": "Shut in by stupendous mountains which rest on crags that tower more than a thousand feet above the water, whose rugged brows and shadowy breaks are clothed by dark and tangled woods, they have such an aspect of deep seclusion, of utter and unbroken solitude, that, when standing on their brink a lonely traveler, I was overwhelmed with an emotion of the sublime, such as I have rarely felt. It was not that the jagged precipices were lofty, that the encircling woods were of the dimmest shade, or that the waters were profoundly deep; but that over all, rocks, wood, and water, brooded the spirit of repose, and the silent energy of nature stirred the soul to its inmost depths."

Franconia Notch has survived extinction twice. In the 1920s the notch was threatened with clear-cut logging (winner take all). A national outpouring of editorials, poems, and money rescued the notch. Donations came from bankers and women's clubs; children at an orphanage sent in their pennies. Franconia Notch was set aside as a state park. Then, in the 1950s, the notch was threatened again, this time with an interstate highway. The blasting and filling for four lanes and shoulders and access ramps would have overwhelmed the narrow notch and buried parts of Echo and Profile Lakes, squeezing what was left behind retaining walls. After twenty years of court challenges, studies, and new federal laws, a declawed two-lane "parkway" edition of the interstate slips through the notch, not much bigger than the old state route it replaced. It was a great victory. This is the only place in the 46,876 miles of interstate where the mandated four-lane highway was overturned. Today we have a scenic highway, a tamed landscape, still beautiful, but the spirit that moved Cole and many other artists has walked away.

I chi-go, I chi-e the Japanese say—"one encounter, one opportunity" or "one time, one meeting"—one of the many Japanese expressions, tricky to translate, for the fleetingness of life, for the way moments arise and are gone. *I chi-go, I chi-e*—"for this time only."

Willey House

The Willey House in Crawford Notch made the White Mountains famous. In 1826 the Willey family was caught in an avalanche. They ran out of their house—the lone house for miles around—only to be killed. Their house was untouched. Had they stayed home they would have lived. The family of seven, plus two hired hands, died. The bodies of three children were never found. This story captivated people for years, figuring in stories, poems, and sermons. Tourists visited the house, which sat as the Willeys had left it, with the Bible open on the table. Everyone was ready with a moral about the strength of the family hearth and the Lord's mysterious ways. The house was one of the White Mountains' most popular tourist attractions until it burned down in 1899.

In engravings and paintings the Willey House is starkly surrounded by huge boulders on a steep hillside. It looks forlorn and unforgiving. The engravings are meant to make the viewer gasp: *How could anyone live there?*

The Willey House site, marked by the Daughters of the American

Revolution (DAR) in 1925, is in a flat place right by a souvenir stand and bathrooms. What you see is a brown souvenir stand with an air conditioner sticking out the window close upon the DAR-marked foundation, which has a footprint about the size of a toolshed. Behind it is a telltale white cane, a vent pipe for a septic field, and behind that, bathrooms.

The souvenir stand is retro-tacky, summer-camp rustic. Inside there are cute little souvenirs with bears and moose, a few booklets about the Willey family disaster, ice cream, and a big display of many-flavored fudge.

The Willey House site says, "A family died here. Would you like some fudge?" That's the story I get from our visit. We had a hard time accepting this as the site of this wilderness tragedy.

The Willey disaster never coheres into a myth, to a clear story, to "essences" beyond human complexity, as Roland Barthes said. It's muddled. The nineteenth-century storytellers and moralists wanted it to become a fable, to pass into a new-forming American myth. But it was just upsetting: a panicked family rushing out into the night to die.

Cathedral Ledge

The ledge was a favorite of the nineteenth-century landscape painters. You would be hard pressed to find most of their viewpoints, which have been subsumed by a monster-sized case of sprawl. We tried, poking around behind outlet malls and near a fantasy adventure motel. (Your choice of rooms: Log Cabin, Roman Spa, The Jungle, Dragon's Lair, Deserted Island, 1970s Love Shack, New York Penthouse, Motorcycle Madness, among others.) We looked off a famous hill and found one view near a banana hut–themed water slide. Here, in the summer of 1850, John Frederick Kensett made the sketches for what would become an iconic view of the young nation, *Mount Washington from the Valley of Conway,* with the great mountain seen across the valley known as the Intervale. The American Art Union bought the painting the next year and circulated an engraving to its thirteen thousand five hundred members. Artists set out for the Intervale. "The meadows and the banks of the Saco were dotted all about with white umbrellas in great numbers," recalled Kensett's close friend and painting companion Benjamin Champney, noting the umbrellas that shaded painting easels. Currier & Ives altered Kensett's painting (recasting Mount Washington as a Swiss Alp), making it the most popular American landscape painting in the nineteenth century.

"This view from Intervale can not be surpassed for living, glowing beauty by anything in New England," said Champney. "The view has been painted many times and by artists of great distinction, but never has the ideal been realized. Its elusive charm can not be fully grasped."

Starr King agreed, praising the valley and the village of North Conway. "Such profuse and calm beauty sometimes reigns over the whole village, that it seems to be ... a suburb of Paradise. ... Certainly, we have seen no other region of New England that is so swathed in dreamy charm."

The broad valley bewitched artists. Their love for the Intervale shows. Their paintings carry you into the valley's Sunday quiet. In hundreds of paintings, the Intervale provided a bucolic foreground and middleground to Mount Washington. Along the Saco's curving riverbanks, cows grazed under elms. The land was as soft and open as the English countryside, a contrast to the rough profile of Mount Washington in the distance.

Champney painted the Intervale many times, as well as other grand mountain scenes, but his favorite place was the Artists' Brook near his summer home. "From the first day I sketched ... I have never ceased to be loyal to my first love. Many, many days and hours have I passed, painting and singing an accompaniment to its silvery music," he said. He knew "almost every nook and transparent pool in its three-mile course." He'd set out with his lunch in his pocket and his "trap," his paints, easel, and canvases, to work in "some secluded, solitary point, with no voice but the brook to cheer me or urge me on to the struggle of solving Nature's mysteries of light and shade and color."

If you were looking for a prescription for how to live, this would be it. We could all do well by being Benjamin Champney at Artists' Brook. Live local, look deeply; realize the impossibility of ever really knowing even a few square inches of the earth. Sing the joys of your place, over and over, knowing that you can never get it right.

"These have been the most happy days, for the striving to do a difficult thing is most pleasurable, even though the work is not successful," Champney said. This is what artists know. "Artists, by the nature of their work, are solitary," James wrote for a catalog to one of his shows. "Our most important hours are invisible to the public, days of quiet work, both exultant and tortured. We are judged not by our effort but by the end product . . . the art. But most art is not entirely successful; it only points the way for improving on the next attempt. A painting is only finished when there is nothing else one can do to make it any better. True success is simply starting again, striving for something ineffable, unrealized and unimagined."

∾

We drove to the top of Cathedral Ledge, where there were three oddities:

* A low chain-link fence near the edge. It is probably the only fence on any of the thousands of ledges, cliffs, and overlooks in New Hampshire.

* A sign:

Do Not
Throw Objects
Rock Climbers Below

* The rock climbers, who clanged like Marley's ghost as they tied themselves to a spindly tree worn smooth from so many ropes, hopped the low fence and dropped out of sight.

James surveyed the Intervale below. On one farm, an old-timer on an old red tractor was making hay. In the next field, migrants working, backs bent, were picking strawberries. In the forest was the beach of a state park, which even at this distance looked trodden. Overused and underfunded. Directly below, the forest was cut into lots. A-frame houses. Vacationland! The wide, sandy banks of the Saco River curved through the valley. Across the way as the hills climbed were a sandpit, a ski resort, and a platoon of condos—long gray slots in the green.

James got that lemon-tasting look on his face. "Forget it," was all he said as he turned away. He looked seriously disappointed, like a captain disgusted by a false report of a landfall.

"It's closed to us," he said. "What those early painters saw is closed to us."

"It is," I agreed. "On this day, at this moment, it's closed to us."

We left. Back in the valley we stopped at a drive-through strawberry stand. (We got out of the car.) On our way to our last stop we passed a mobile-home dealership that featured a log-cabin model. A log cabin on wheels. There's a lot of American history right there: The frontier on the road. Daniel Boone meets Jack Kerouac. *Little House at the Gas Pump.*

What did we see? I have a one-word answer: motion.

We saw traffic. We saw people in their motor-home community, so friendly over breakfast, so ready to pack and roll. Community divisible in ten minutes.

We saw obese children on little motorbikes.

We saw cars and motorcycles zooming up a mountain.

We saw people in ropes and gear throwing themselves off a cliff.

We saw a drive-through strawberry stand.

We saw a log-cabin mobile home.

We saw mountains scarred for ski runs.

We saw motion.

We kept moving.

The old order was a walker's pace. Even after the railroad had delivered the tourists to their hotels, they spent much of their time walking the piazza and nearby trails or on horseback or in a carriage. The grand hotels were a European transplant, an echo of the Old Country in an immigrant nation. The North Country has never gotten over the grand hotel era. They have spent a long time thinking about when they held the world's attention as "the Switzerland of America." Everywhere you go in the White Mountains you are confronted with souvenirs of past glory, historic signs and dates on buildings, and photos of vanished hotels.

The new order is American. The interstate highway wedged right into Franconia Notch. Zoom and go and go some more. During Laconia Motorcycle Week in June, which brings a couple hundred thousand motorcycles into New Hampshire, my wife and I were far up a trail in Franconia Notch, by a waterfall. We couldn't escape the motorcycles' pulsing song.

Americans are not a people who sit in mountainside teahouses and write haiku or paint or do calligraphy. Faced with a big landscape, with a big place, we increase our rpm—we go, go, go. We up our gear—big motor homes with stuff hung on the side or top: kayaks, mountain bikes, motorbikes, and a car or all-terrain vehicle in tow. Draped in piles of dangling carabiners like modern chain mail, we throw ourselves over rock ledges. We dress in leather and Kevlar pants and motorcycle, or bright yellow jerseys and Lycra pants and bicycle.

We don't look at landscapes. We move through them.

Motion. Not emotion.

The auto road is a monument to motion, to the crazy American refusal to accept the end of the road. Drive on.

As James had watched the cars going up and down the Mount Washington Auto Road, he'd almost had vertigo, he said. The mountain seemed trivialized as an amusement ride. He was saddened by what he had seen, by the lack of "rest" in the rest area.

"It's the sadness of not arriving," I said. *You are here*—but you are not. You are in transit. Where is *here*? The signs tell you, the exhibits, all trying to make up for the disconnection. Most tourist places are defined by an accumulation of narrative: signs, pamphlets, and exhibits. Explanation or, rather, "information" is the mark of a tourist site. Everything will be explained: What you are looking at, why you are looking at it, and the best place to pose for a photo in front of it. You are *not* here and soon you are gone. On to the next attraction. There is no smack in our seeing.

~

We didn't drive up the mountain that summer day. We returned in winter. James booked two seats for us in the snowcat, the giant snowplow that clears the road in winter. The summit that day wasn't home to "the world's worst weather"; it was having a fine, blue-sky day. We could see for more than a hundred miles—mountains in all directions. The view, James said, is all distance. There's no middle ground; the foreground is created by having someone stand in front. We were looking at space. Mountains without end. No narrative. We couldn't shuffle the deck and make it tell stories.

The summit is choked with narration, with the histories of the Tip-Top House, the stage office, and signs and markers and tales of different climbs, different peaks we could see from there. Supplying this history is the equivalent of trying to make up for the lack of foreground and middle ground in the view. It's an attempt to add our scale, our size. The same can be said of the paintings and guidebooks whose mission is to get what we see into a shape we can understand: beginning, middle, end; foreground, middle ground, background. Let's put the human eye in the equation and let's put our sense of narrative here. Let's make a clock we can read.

But nothing in the mountains is moving to the timeline of our short lives. The mountains are millions of years old, having arisen as continents drifted and collided. They rose up and up, were scoured by ice for millennia, and stand here today in this brief moment between ice ages.

The sublime was about glimpsing that other timeline, a view into eternity or, as Emerson said, "an influx of the Divine Mind into our mind." The artist's task, said Cole, was to teach people "the laws by which the Eternal doth sublime and sanctify his works, that we may see the hidden glory veiled from vulgar eyes."

Is all our activity—the auto road, hiking, rock climbing, driving all-terrain vehicles into the woods—an attempt to shout down the sublime? To turn mountains into selfies? Or is it what we do to fill a void, the void where the sublime was?

All the paintings, the mountains bearing the names of presidents and scrambled Indian legends, the historical markers, all of this is an effort to domesticate a place, to make a wilderness more homelike. It's an attempt to make ourselves visible amid the mountains. To declare a view sublime or beautiful is also to downsize the mountains, to get a frame around them. The paintings are stories and the stories they tell are of mountains that are there for us—to uplift, to instruct, to thrill—but all for us.

So much of our activity is about naming. In the early 1800s, Lucy Crawford guided many climbing parties up Mount Washington. She was a skilled host; she ran an inn with her family. She knew what her guests wanted; that's why she went through the trouble of carrying up the mountain a large sheet of lead, "eight or ten feet in length, seven inches wide, and the thickness of pasteboard." It was for her guests to write their names on with an iron pencil she had made. This was much quicker than waiting for everyone to pound their names into the summit with a hammer and chisel. Her hiking parties often stayed only long enough to carve their names, just long enough to downsize the mountain with their story. All the historical markers and photos, all the applications of history is foreground—it's carving our names.

Here's a vast landscape, one that it's easy enough to die in, so we throw dates and narrative at the big mountains. It's a way of creating foreground, of pushing the mountains back. We can't inhabit the vast mountain itself, even on the top of Mount Washington with all its buildings.

∼

The early visitors to the White Mountains delighted in echoes. Innkeepers would fire off a gun or a cannon in Crawford Notch to entertain their guests. Guidebooks would direct hikers to the better echo points, such as Mount Agassiz, where at the right spot, they could hear the mountain returning their call five times. There are two Echo Lakes, only forty-five miles apart. "These mountains are full of echoes. There are 'echo lakes' and 'echo hills' and echo places unnumbered," reported the newspaper published on Mount Washington's summit, *Among the Clouds,* in 1877. In Franconia Notch, the firing of a cannon was part of the ritual of visiting that Echo Lake. The echoes broke the silence; the mountains spoke to them.

What we want to find in the mountains is everything that's missing in the valleys—freedom, adventure, a new self, a new earth. The hope is that a sheer rise of rock, a new angle of light, will liberate us from ourselves.

∼

Driving home, James was thinking about what it takes to make a "lump of rock" mean something to humans.

After discussing this for many miles, we more or less agree that a good painting makes the unseen visible, and once visible, the painting buries it. The scene becomes obscured by what people have been taught to see. Expectations are clouding the view. The real thing is covered over by an image that is diluted in reproductions, postcards, mugs, tote bags, and with words and analysis. The mountain view disappears. It becomes a sign, a representation of itself—something we recognize in a blink, in an outline.

Great art promises liberation, contact with the real, but ends up, too often, as yet another obstruction to seeing. The progression of our visits to art museums sadly mimics the rise and fall of seeing. We confront the works of art and spill out into the gift shop where the art is reduced to a signature painting or part of a painting on a shopping bag—a sign of a sign.

"To see is to forget the name of the thing one sees," said Paul Valery. But naming the thing, painting the thing, is to forget seeing. Like a leviathan, the mountain view rises from the deep, is seen, is named, and then disappears.

SEEKING FREEDOM

Crossing Over, Crossing Back

I. Crossing Over

A lbert Johnston was one of two Black students in his class at the University of Chicago's Rush Medical College in 1929. That was the quota: two. To become a doctor, a student had to intern at a hospital. But no white hospitals allowed Negro or colored doctors, as it was said then. In the entire country there were four Black hospitals that accepted interns, and his school said he couldn't intern at any of them. They had put Albert in an impossible situation, given him an unsolvable puzzle. If he couldn't solve this puzzle, his medical career would be over before it began. Medicine, said the *Chicago Defender*, one of the country's leading Black newspapers, was "the most Jim Crowed profession in American life."

He applied to hospitals that he thought might be liberal. Toledo wanted him, until he showed up for his interview and was told they didn't accept colored interns. The same thing happened in Worcester, Massachusetts, where he arrived after scraping together the money for the trip. While in medical school, he worked part time as a railroad porter and dining-car waiter or at nights in the post office.

He was already married, and he had a young son. His wife, Thyra, was living with her parents in Boston. At last, after thirty-one rejections, a hospital in Portland, Maine, asked him to come for an interview. Thyra bought him a suit and some ties at a pawn shop.

They liked the young man and hired him. They hadn't asked about his race, and he hadn't said anything. Soon Albert was out to dinner and playing tennis with the other interns. People liked Albert. He was, he knew, "a good mixer." Once he was there, no one bothered the young intern about his race. "You know when you first came we thought you might be a Filipino, or maybe Hawaiian, or a Jew," they said later. "We didn't know what you were," but, it was implied, they could overlook that. They could allow one Filipino or Hawaiian or Jew.

And with that, Dr. Johnston had passed for white. Puzzle solved; new puzzle created. He hadn't wanted to pass, to "cross over." In medical school, he belonged to the Negro fraternity. He was light skinned, as was Thyra, who had light brown hair and blue eyes. He was, by his own reckoning, more than one-third Black, and Thyra was one-eighth. Albert was born in Chicago. His father grew up on a Michigan farm; his people had not been slaves. His mother's parents had been enslaved in Mississippi. His father was lighter than Albert, and he passed to work as a real estate agent. Thyra Baumann was born in New Orleans, where her German grandfather had married a Black woman. Her father was a clerk at the post office. When she was nine years old, her family fled the segregated South, ending up in Boston. The Baumanns also passed as white. They had white friends and, separately, Black friends in Boston's small community of Black lawyers, doctors, and dentists.

Thyra's parents were anxious about whom she dated. They thwarted her romance with a Black football player from Brown University, refusing to let her go to the big game against Harvard with a group of his Black friends for fear she might be seen. "My dad was very fair and handsome. He said he had brought us up out of New Orleans to get us out of it," said Thyra. "My parents felt that if I married a dark man, I would be 'going back.'" They hid the football player's love letters. "I couldn't understand why I didn't hear from him," said Thyra. When she fell in love with Albert, her parents had to see what this medical student looked like. Thyra was visiting friends in Chicago for a couple of weeks when she met Albert. He proposed and asked her to stay. She went to look for work. Her mother sent a telegram and then called: come home immediately. Thyra did as she was told. So Albert wrote, sent telegrams, and called. He went to Boston on his Christmas break. Her parents approved, and they were married a short time later.

～

Dr. Johnston was now white or Filipino or Jewish, whatever people chose to see. When Thyra got a job as a stenographer, she put "white" on the job application, and also Protestant. The company didn't hire Blacks or Catholics like herself. To get the job, she wore the required disguise.

"America is a land of masking jokers," wrote Ralph Ellison. "Americans began their revolt from the English fatherland when they dumped the tea into the harbor, masked as Indians," and we've been choosing masks "for good and evil ever since," he said. Benjamin Franklin "allowed the French to mistake him for Rousseau's Natural Man. . . . Abe Lincoln allowed himself to be taken for a simple country lawyer." For Blacks, wearing the mask is a "profound rejection of the image created to usurp his identity. Sometimes it is for the sheer joy of the joke," to put one over on the whites, to evade the cruelties of Jim Crow. "Change the joke and slip the yoke," said Ellison. "Masking is a play upon possibility and ours is a society in which possibilities are many." Or to borrow a phrase of the time, passing gave Albert Johnston "a white man's chance."

He had done so well as an intern that the hospital chief offered him a position as a pathologist, and the head of the board of registration, which licensed doctors, suggested that he look into buying the thriving practice of a small-town doctor who had just died. The possibilities were many for the young doctor.

He went to look at the practice, driving north almost a hundred miles into the White Mountains of New Hampshire to Gorham, a town of just over twenty-seven hundred crossed by the Appalachian Trail. Many people worked in the forest or in the paper mills in town or nearby. The doctor's widow welcomed him. She would sell him the practice for $1,000, rent him her husband's office, and field his phone calls. The local bank was also welcoming, ready to loan him $2,000 to get set up.

Dr. Johnston was a busy country doctor, called out at three on a winter's morning when it was far below zero, delivering babies, visiting feverish children, pulling teeth, setting the broken leg of a dog. He was paid sometimes with cash and sometimes with eggs, butter, and vegetables, or not paid at all, and he would send no bill—it was, after all, hard times, the Great Depression of the 1930s.

The town took to the young doctor and his growing family. The Congregational minister invited them to join the church and send their children to Sunday school. Albert was elected to the school board and joined the Rotary Club and the Masonic Lodge. He was a selectman, a basketball coach, chair of the local Republican Party, and president of the county medical society. "I can't remember all the things he was president of," said Thyra. He was president of just about everything. She was president of the Gorham Woman's Club and the White Mountain Junior League. She hosted teas and small parties, and with Albert played bridge with other couples, sometimes competing in state tournaments.

But the Johnstons were wary. Despite their success, they continued to rent a house and not buy one so they could leave town in a hurry if they had to. There was a klavern of the Ku Klux Klan in town, though they never looked twice at the Johnstons—who they thought were white— or at Abe Stahl, the town's one Jew, an elderly German immigrant who lived on Main Street. The Klan in New Hampshire directed its hatred at Catholics, especially the French-speaking Canadians working in the mills.

The Johnstons guarded their identity; that is the hard work of passing. They didn't allow their friends or their darker relatives to visit. When they went to Boston to see family and friends, they never took their children. In time, old friends and some relatives fell away.

And for all that, Gorham felt like home. When they decided to buy a house after being there five years, the town sold them a showplace, the

George Washington Noyes House up on Prospect Terrace overlooking Main Street. Gorham had owned the Noyes House for years, since the last owners had defaulted on their mortgage. "The citizens wanted to be sure they had only the *best* people living there—no Jews or Catholics, for example—so they sold to us at a ridiculous price! They seemed to think that since we were Protestant and white, we were just right," Albert said years later.

The Noyes House was a big, three-story Victorian in the Queen Anne style with an octagonal tower and a mix of gables, dormers, bay windows, clapboards and shingles, open and enclosed porches, and an attached barn. The house had seventeen rooms, including a large reception hall for parties. The Johnstons hosted the church's Christmas social and a New Year's reception. Everyone in town went to these parties; they had the most popular house in town. The Congregational church put its Christmas tree in their yard. These were happy years.

Gorham was home, with good friends and people who admired the Johnstons, but it was a home founded on uncertainty. There was always a worry that their secret would be found out. Once, Thyra's father, who looked white, was visiting, waiting on the riverbank while the family was swimming, when a stranger said, "See that lady down there? Well, they say she's a real mulattress. But, now, funny thing is, her husband's darker'n what she is." Her father replied, "You must be very much mistaken, because that lady is my daughter." You could be president of everything, live in one of the town's best houses, throw the best and biggest parties; you could be respected and even loved, and yet, how deep did all that run? It all came down to "and yet." Gorham was home, he was a beloved doctor, and yet.

Albert wasn't content to be a country doctor; he wanted to specialize. A nearby hospital needed a radiologist, so he moved his family to Boston for a year while he studied roentgenology in a postgraduate program at the Harvard Medical School, the first Black ever in the program, as far as he knew, though he was admitted as white. At Harvard, Albert was known as "the Baron" for his ability to spin a good story, said Thyra. "And everybody in the department would say, 'Doctor, that can't be true.'" Albert would answer, "'Oh yes, indeed, that's true—that's the way they say it up in New England.' He had a good sense of humor." He was a good mixer.

In Boston, their oldest son, Albert Jr., who was eleven years old with olive-toned skin, experienced prejudice for the first time. Some of the other kids in school thought he was Jewish. He ran into prejudice again at prep school a few years later when his roommate taunted him by constantly asking, "What *are* you?" A Jew? Greek? *What?*—A Negro? Albert Jr. didn't know he was Black. As a boy, he saw a Black man once when a tramp spent the night in the Gorham jail. He and his friends went down to the jail to look at the man. "We'd never seen one before. It was strange to us," he said.

"What are we going to do when the children grow up?" Thyra asked her husband.

"Maybe we won't have to do anything. Let's just saw wood and see what happens," he said.

They had been back in Gorham for two years when a good opportunity came along for a radiologist at a hospital in Keene, a small city of more than thirteen thousand in the southwest corner of the state, over toward Vermont. They were reluctant to leave Gorham, where even the dogs knew Dr. Johnston so well that they didn't bark when he made his house calls.

Keene was a larger place, suffused with the chill of the distance Yankees kept from strangers. It took about a decade for folks to get know you, it was said, and you'd always be from someplace else, a flatlander. The ladies from the Congregational church called on Thyra early, but it wasn't like Gorham. The Johnstons rented a house again, and after three years felt secure enough to buy it, an imposing three-story brick Federal-style home with thirteen rooms on one of the city's best streets. It could have fit right in on the campuses of New England's oldest colleges. They were active once more in the church and various civic organizations, and they made new friends. Their family had grown to four children, with one girl, Anne, the second oldest. Anne was voted most popular in her high-school class. She was a cheerleader and a class vice president. Her brother Donald managed the high-school football team, played hockey, and was in the band and the drama club.

There was one other Black family in town. George Miller managed the larger of Keene's two movie theaters. Miller's family, his wife and daughter, were popular. Keene is "one of the most liberal cities in the world," he said. His family had never experienced discrimination, but that may have been because Blacks were rare in northern New England. When a Black chauffeur showed up on the city's Central Square, the common at the head of Main Street, a group of children gathered to stare.

Under Dr. Johnston, the Radiology Department at Elliot Community Hospital grew rapidly. He succeeded at anything he tried. With World War II coming on, he was sure that he could help his country. The navy wrote to him twice, offering him a commission. The military desperately needed doctors. Radiologists were in demand—for the first time, every inductee would be X-rayed. There were only twenty-five hundred radiologists in the country, and many were old or essential for their communities. In April 1941, eight months before the attack on Pearl Harbor, Dr. Johnston applied to the Naval Reserve.

He knew that the navy, like the rest of the armed forces, was segregated. There were no Black officers. Blacks served mainly as mess attendants. He also knew that the navy would thoroughly investigate him. "I'd be exposed all around," he told Thyra. But "if the navy does accept me, people can say what they like about us, but we will have given our children a real background." The navy, a racist institution, would be certifying Dr. Johnston as white.

[95]

He went to Boston for a physical exam. He was interviewed by the director of Naval Reserve and by the district medical officer. The navy accepted him. He was overweight and an inch and a half short, but they waived those "physical defects." Albert Johnston was commissioned as a lieutenant commander and assigned to a unit in the Medical Corps of the Naval Reserve. Dr. Johnston was now a white naval officer. "And now we won't need ever tell the children anything," he told his wife.

But the navy was still investigating. They discovered what was right out in the open: at college, Albert had belonged to a Negro fraternity. The navy's intelligence bureau sent a young investigator to Keene with just one question:

"We understand that, even though you are registered as white, you have colored blood in your veins."

"Who knows what blood any of us has in our veins," replied the doctor, who had looked inside thousands of people.

"Thank you very much, doctor. That's all we want to know." The young man was polite. He left.

Three weeks later, Albert received a letter rescinding his commission. He had failed "to meet naval physical requirements," they said, noting his weight and height. He was upset by this news, but determined. He lost forty pounds and applied again. He was denied again. His height was "still a disqualifying defect," they said.

After that the doctor tried everything to serve his country. He tried the army. He tried to get appointed to the "colored" troops. He had influential friends arguing for him. He wrote to the surgeon general, to the Office for Emergency Management, and to the War Manpower Commission. He took his case to the secretary of war via a civilian aide, a man who had served as the first Black federal judge and might be sympathetic. No one would have him. After his great popularity in Gorham and Harvard, his success in Keene, this rejection hurt the Baron. "I could just about cry for him over that," said his son, Albert Jr.

All the while, the American Board of Radiology was sending him letters, urging him to volunteer to meet the need for experienced radiologists. The navy also wrote, more frequently as war went on. In 1942:

> Dear Friend,
> You have no doubt wondered just what you could do personally to be of assistance in the war efforts of our country. . . . May I suggest a way you can render a real service?

The letter suggested that he serve in a company of "Negro tradesmen" based in Alabama. They needed carpenters, electricians, machinists, firemen, and so forth. The forty-two-year-old doctor may have never picked up a hammer in his life.

The day he received the last of a long train of rejections, Albert Jr. came home from prep school full of praise for his friend Charlie. "Everyone liked Charlie, even if he is colored," said Albert Jr. His father sat him down for a serious talk.

II. Crossing Back

Here's the Johnston family in 1952, after the war, after all the children had been told their heritage. Here they are in the pages of *Ebony* magazine. The doctor sits by the fireplace of their grand home. He's wearing a suit and tie, reading a book, "the latest race novel," insists *Ebony*. Thyra sits on the other side of the fireplace. She's wearing a black dress, knitting as she smiles at her husband. Their dog, a boxer, sits between them. (The only "pureblooded member" of the family, Albert joked. We're sure he's "100 percent redblooded Boxer.") In the next photo, their son Donald, married to his "white high school girlfriend," is showing Thyra their newborn daughter, her first grandchild. Other photos show the doctor examining an X-ray film as his "white laboratory assistant" looks on; the doctor returning home carrying a classic doctor's bag; Thyra gardening; Albert with a broad smile, bantering with the owner of Keene's camera shop; and the Johnstons "entertaining friends at home." Everyone is dressed formally as their

"European-born" friend "displays his continental aplomb pouring burgundy." (Though the bottle, wrapped in a cloth napkin, and the glasses suggest it's champagne.)

Ebony was the *Life* magazine for the Black community. It was a rallying cry: we're achieving. In that magazine, the Johnstons' presence said: look at us, we're doing our part to uplift the race. *Ebony* presented "chronicles of achievement and admiration, sought, won, thwarted, denied," says Margo Jefferson in her memoir *Negroland*. "*Life* and *Look* affirm and defend norms they are sure of; in *Ebony* we strive to establish norms and be lauded for those we maintain."

Any achievement is precarious, Jefferson says. "Society can turn any success of ours into a setback; permit us to advance, then insist that we fail or, on pain of death, retreat." There was turmoil behind the posed photos of the Johnstons, and *Ebony* talked about some of that, too. The article followed the route of "achievement and admiration, sought, won, thwarted, denied." The Johnstons had been through some tough years.

Albert Jr. was getting ready for a date on the night his father told him. He was running water for a bath and had just told his father what a good guy his friend Charlie was. That comment angered his father. "Turn off the water," he said. "Do you know something, boy?"

"No, what?"

"Well, you're colored."

Albert Jr. felt a "funny sensation" run through him. He looked closely at himself in the mirror. "Well, how come?" he asked. His father told him their family history and how he had to pass. He must not tell anyone, not even his younger siblings. His mother asked him how he felt now that he knew. He said he was proud of his heritage, and that "he hoped to do something for the Negro." But he was stunned. He would have to rethink everything he knew or had assumed. He did not go out on a date that night.

He returned to prep school on a wobbly course. He was a senior on the honor roll, sixteenth in his class, captain of the ski team, assistant yearbook editor, in the choir and the glee club. But now everything was different—or was it? He didn't know how his classmates would react if they knew. He didn't know what it meant to be black, whether he could still go to all the places he usually went, or what jobs he could have. He stopped dating. Any time he thought of calling a girl, he froze—What if she knew? His grades fell. He broke out in a rash that the doctors couldn't cure. They thought it was a "nervous rash." He had a student job in the Admissions Office. He began to wonder if there was a quota. His friend Charlie had been admitted, but suppose twenty or thirty qualified Blacks had applied, would they be admitted? He was obsessed with this question. By the time he left prep school he was in "an awful state," he said.

He was accepted at Dartmouth, but he felt out of place. The other students were wealthy, spending money freely. He couldn't afford to sit in on their poker games. Albert Jr. was waiting tables. They were training for commissions in the army and the navy. He had seen his father denied. He was confused. He would climb a high tower, the only place he believed he could study, and think of jumping to his death. He had a nervous breakdown. His father took him out of school and off to see the first Black psychiatrist.

Albert Jr. tumbled through many jobs in the next few years. He worked at the post office for a few weeks. He enlisted in the navy as white. He did so well on the tests the navy wanted him to train as a radio operator, but he feared that might require investigating his background, so he refused. He ended up scrubbing decks all day. With all that time to think, "the whole bottom seemed to fall out of my stomach and I began shaking, not knowing what I was afraid of." He had another nervous breakdown. The navy hospitalized him in the "nut house." He was discharged as a "psychoneurotic unclassified."

He returned home and moped around the house, listening to the same Paul Robeson record over and over. He took up the piano, which he had not touched in years, playing all day and into the night sometimes, often playing the same notes endlessly. His family got him a job in an ink factory in town, but he got nervous and quit. "I was scared of people and I didn't know why," he said.

His father had reached his limit. He once had great hopes for this son who was brilliant and perceptive; now he worried that his son was "too weak to stand up to life." He lined up all the necessary papers to have his son committed for treatment at a veterans' hospital. Thyra wouldn't allow it; she was furious.

Albert Jr. left home with a friend to hitchhike across America to see how Blacks lived. They thumbed rides and hopped freight trains. He visited his aunts, uncles, and cousins in Cleveland, Chicago, and Los Angeles, where he got an eye-opening education as he met successful Black doctors, lawyers, engineers, and merchants. Growing up he'd heard only "all the bad things you usually hear" about Blacks. He was hosted at fancy parties. He met many others who were mixed race. He was not alone in the world. Looking back from Los Angeles, having crossed the Rockies and the desert riding in boxcars, Keene, New Hampshire, seemed very small and very white. He came home, and after working as a soda jerk and fighting more with his father, he returned to college to study music at the University of New Hampshire, and he began to find his way.

∼

Albert Jr. was eager "to do something for the Negro." With the one other Black male undergraduate at the university, he attended a student conference that passed a resolution calling for there to be movies about Blacks who had "made a contribution," like the scientist George Washington Carver. All you saw in the movies were the most demeaning stereotypes—servants, shoe-shine boys, cotton pickers, "mammies," buffoons, and "Uncle Toms."

Albert Jr. and his friend managed to get an appointment to see an Oscar-winning director who lived just down the road from the university. Louis de Rochemont was famous for making the March of Time newsreels everyone saw at the movies before the main feature. In those pre-television days, this is where people first saw Hitler preparing for war as early as 1935, sharecroppers picking cotton in the South, the Dust Bowl, a New Orleans jazz band, and Franklin Delano Roosevelt being sworn in for his four terms in office, in reports mixing staged scenes with actual footage. ("It's terrific," said *Time's* chief Henry Luce when he viewed the first reels, "but what is it?") De Rochemont was an imposing figure. A non-stop worker "with a shock of disorderly brown hair and the haggard look of an overworked city editor, he fairly explodes with impatient energy," said *Reader's Digest* magazine. "Sleep and rest don't figure in his schedule," said an associate. "He turns every job into a major adventure and all the time he talks your ear off about some new enthusiasm." Most of all, he had "velocity, a gigantic, unmodulated kind of energy" that was like "a maddened elephant crashing through the underbrush at Time, Incorporated," said film historian Raymond Fielding. De Rochemont had a contract with a big Hollywood studio, MGM, that let him choose the films he would produce, and he had a deal with *Reader's Digest* to develop stories that could later be filmed.

The two students told him their idea. "Bio pics" about white men like the inventors Thomas Edison and Alexander Graham Bell were popular; why not make a movie about Carver or the reformer Booker T. Washington? De Rochemont listened politely, and looking at the two students, one who was obviously Black, he asked, "Mr. Johnston, how come you're interested in this?"

"Well, I didn't know I was Black" until recently, Albert Jr. said.

"Is that right?" said de Rochemont.

After Albert Jr. told his story, the director asked him if he could write an eight-page synopsis and get his family's permission for a *Reader's Digest* article, a book, and a movie. "When I called my father at home, he thought maybe I'd been out on a beer bust or something—he didn't understand what was happening," said Albert Jr. He hitchhiked home.

His father was opposed to airing their secret before millions of people. His mother was tired of passing; she wanted the story out. By this point they had told all their children. Albert and Thyra were up all night debating. "It was my decision," Thyra said years later. "We were tired of hiding. It was time to tell our story."

"Lost Boundaries" appeared in *Reader's Digest* in December 1947, followed the next year by a bestselling book. De Rochemont was working on the movie. *Reader's Digest* was America's most popular magazine and, worldwide, was second only to the Bible. The Johnstons' secret belonged to the public.

Our friends in Keene, said Thyra, "came to see us, sent us cards and flowers and we weren't quite sure whether they were congratulating us or condoling with us."

The story rattled some of the Johnstons' relatives who did not know they were black. After the story appeared, Albert received an unsigned letter:

> I am a white man, happen to be married to a relative of yours— again please forgive names. My wife . . . has been proud of your grandfather . . . I am sure it would kill her to know the truth, if it is the truth about him. . . . Tragedy would certainly result should she find out what I have read in *Reader's Digest*.
>
> I cannot believe that any concerned with this story meant it to be harmful or malicious. That would be criminal, hence I am appealing to you. . . . We have a girl baby, and another on the way. You can understand my concern in the matter, I hope. Personally I have no prejudices in the matter, but you can readily understand my interest. . . . Others connected in the family might not be as broadminded as I am. Surely you would wish no harm or tragedies to enter into their lives, especially since it will do no harm to omit certain passages in the forthcoming book.

～

Passing is loss. Crossing over is a "chosen exile," says historian Allyson Hobbs. A person passing out of the Black community leaves an absence, a break in the family tree, and gaps in the family photo albums. People usually talk about what is gained by passing, but they seldom talk about the losses, she says. It's a kind of divorce, a wholesale erasing of family history. A discarded nephew or niece may only learn of an aunt's or uncle's funeral by reading the newspaper. Their attendance at the funeral would shatter the family's image of whiteness. "The core issue of passing," says Hobbs, "is not becoming what you pass for, but losing what you pass from."

To pass is to never be able to go home again, to avert your eyes when another black is nearby, to "cut them," to not acknowledge them. Your life is based on a secret, one that your relatives and your old neighbors won't break. They may simultaneously root for you to put the joke over and disdain you as a traitor to your race. Simple things could undo you, like mail from relatives in Black neighborhoods, so you may have two addresses to segregate your mail, to manage your divided self. You have worries unimagined in the white world. If you fall sick at work, you can't let a colleague drive you home to a Black neighborhood—if you're "working white," passing as white nine-to-five, but still Black at home. The Johnstons had few Black friends, *Ebony* noted.

Passers are seekers exiled in a land their ancestors never chose. They seek relief from daily slights and rejections, restaurants that won't serve them, stores where the clerks follow them around, railroads that segregate them to a dirty "smokers" car, "the catalogue of disaster—the policeman, the taxi driver, the waiters, the landlady, the banks, the insurance companies, the millions of details twenty-four hours of every day which spell out to you that you are a worthless human being," as James Baldwin said in 1965. "It comes as a great shock to discover that the country which is your birthplace and to which you owe your life and identity has not, in its whole system of reality, evolved any place for you," he said. The passer is seeking a place, a job, a house, a fair chance, a "white man's chance." Passers are seeking fairness. That's all. Judge me by the content of my character. They want the Constitution to mean what it says, to be more than words on old parchment. They want it to apply to them. They want respect.

"I am a man. I intend to be recognized as a man and treated with respect," said Dr. Johnston, after his story was out. "If I must be white on occasion to get such respect, I will be white, for nobody shall ever dictate to me how I shall live or where my place in life shall be. I, alone, will determine that!"

Passing had brought him far, and it had tripped him up. Passing stands outside the usual stories about hard work and opportunity. The American Dream is presented as an immigrant's story—rising from nothing, overcoming hatred and poverty, assimilating, and changing the culture. In "a land of masking jokers," as Ellison said, the story of success is a dance of many masks, a pursuit in which the seeker recreates himself, fashions his image, chooses his story, shows up and climbs the ladder. Dr. Johnston had been yanked off the ladder.

The navy's rejection had laid him low. "I guess I've become morose," he said a couple of years after the war. The Baron told a story. There was a music teacher who had dreamed since she was a girl of owning a concert grand piano, the biggest piano made, a piano that commands attention in places like Carnegie Hall. Her dream piano was a special one, too, white with gold legs. She worked for years giving lessons, and finally she bought her dream piano. It was white with gold legs, but it didn't sound anything like the piano in her dreams. It was just another piano.

"I have more or less an empty life. Maybe a little like the white piano with gold legs," he said.

Did this emptiness set in little by little, like a snowfall, or was it an avalanche? Did it hit him one night at the Rotary or the Masons? Did he look around at his fellows in these all-white clubs, these terminally "nice" and "good people" who never tested their supposed goodness against the moral challenges of the day, and did he think, "Is that all there is?" This wasn't the Promised Land.

As a radiologist he had "peered inside of practically everybody" around, he said. He was skilled in interpreting shadows. He'd seen enough. He quit the Rotary, stopped going to the Masonic Lodge. Passing was a project he may have lost interest in. He stayed home; he began to drink.

He would have preferred to have been a Black doctor from the start, but that was not possible for him. And now as he crossed back, he was in a kind of no-man's land. Despite all he had accomplished, he said, "Whatever I do, my race gets no credit."

He had refused to let others define him, to tell him who he was. When James Baldwin was giving a talk to teachers in 1963, he explained that he was not who they thought he was, who white people had been saying he was since he could remember. All the hatred and the ugly slurs, that's your invention, he said. "Because if I am not what I've been told I am, then it means that you're not what you thought you were either! And that is the crisis." But what if I am not who I say I am? That's the passer's dilemma.

III. Dance of the Masking Jokers

Lost Boundaries, the movie, opened in 1949 to good reviews, strong box office, and controversy. It was banned in Atlanta and Memphis— it was incendiary; it "could have created riots in theaters where extremely partisan audiences were in attendance," said Miss Christine Smith, the censor on Atlanta's Library Board. Free speech is a *privilege,* she said; you can't yell fire in a theater. *Lost Boundaries* "contained inferences throughout which created preachments against long-standing customs," meaning Jim Crow. Northerners must understand "the fact that segregation is a matter of law in the south—not just a matter of prejudice," she said. De Rochemont took the censor to court, and the publicity boosted the movie. *Lost Boundaries* played in more than twenty-five cities throughout the South, and for six months in a Broadway theater in New York. After the first showing in New York, when the lights came on, the audience sat in stunned silence. No one moved.

The actor Carleton Carpenter, who played the boyfriend of the

Johnstons' daughter in the movie, remembers that opening night. The audience gasped at some of the lines, and "people were whispering: 'Did he really say that?' 'I heard that.' It was a really shocking film."

It was risky to make. After checking with an "audience research" pollster, MGM backed out. De Rochement produced the film himself, financing it by mortgaging his house, farm, cars, and his film company, and getting backing from two angel investors. The actor Mel Ferrer, who appears as the Doctor Johnston character in the film, was warned by his agent not to take the part because it could jeopardize his career. They "begged me not to do it," he said. This was his first movie, and after it came out, Ferrer was accused of passing. "This was a very radical departure from any kind of fiction film anybody was making in the country. It established a new freedom in making films," said Ferrer. The rest of the cast was worried that it could be too controversial to be released. "We thought we might be making a movie that will never be seen," said Susan Douglas, who played the family's daughter.

Lost Boundaries was "a real breakthrough," says Donald Bogle, a leading scholar of Black cinema. "The Black characters" are "not the old-style Stepin Fetchit figure. These people do not speak with heavy dialects, they are not shuffling. They are composed, dignified, educated people who have a problem in America because of American discrimination and bigotry."

The *New York Times* and *Time* chose it as one of the ten best films of 1949. "Viewed as emotional entertainment, as social enlightenment or both, it is one of the most effective pictures that we are likely to have this year," said the *Times*. It's "not only a first-class social document, but also a profoundly moving film," said *Time*. The film picked up major awards, including one for the best script at the Cannes Film Festival. The NAACP, which was campaigning to get Hollywood's derogatory images off the screen, said it was "certainly the most courageous treatment of the Negro in motion pictures to date."

Lost Boundaries appeared in a year with three other films that took on the issues of race in America. "Nineteen forty nine is definitely lining up as the year of the Negro problem pic," said *Variety*. World War II had exposed the lie at the center of our democracy, the twelve million Americans who were denied their basic rights. Blacks had fought in Europe and the Pacific for the American way and now they wanted real freedom at home. They had been fighting for a "double victory," they said. They had not risked their lives to return to a life as a "half American." The "Double V" campaign was part of the push leading to the integration of baseball in 1947 and the armed forces in 1948. For a short season, Hollywood gambled that audiences were ready to get a little closer to the ugly facts of racism.

Like the other "problem pictures" of 1949, *Lost Boundaries* is a flawed pioneer—flaws that the NAACP and other reviewers were willing to overlook. The film is compromised by having white actors play Blacks, as was common practice then—or more exactly, whites were playing Blacks who were passing as white—it's a traffic pile-up of masking jokers. The white audience, Hollywood believed, could only identify with someone who looked like them. By not casting Black actors, Hollywood was practicing its own segregation, said critics.

"These films are not *about* Negroes at all; they are about what whites think and feel about Negroes," said Ralph Ellison in his review. And there was "much confusion" about what whites thought. *Lost Boundaries,* he argued, evaded the question it raised: Did Dr. Johnston have the right to pass, to choose his mask, his path to success? "For after all, whiteness *has* been given an economic and social value in our culture."

Passing, a fraught subject for both Blacks and whites, was an odd choice to try to advance understanding among the races, say critics and historians like Donald Bogle. The Johnstons' problems are not those of most Blacks. The film "had created a dream situation, an isolated fantasy world no more real than those of all-black musicals," says Bogle. Critics do admire the film, but if they could go back to 1949, this is not where they would have begun the long march for civil rights.

But the Johnstons thought de Rochemont had told their story well. Thyra brushed aside the criticism of the casting. "I say, one thing at a time, and the risk of getting *Lost Boundaries* filmed at all was quite an undertaking," she wrote to de Rochemont just after the film opened. "Had you known of its guaranteed success, no doubt you could have used colored actors, and yet I do think the impact would not have been half so forceful. The public might be reticent to accept everything at one throw, and for that reason I think your judgment was sound. We think you made a great stride."

The reviewers agreed; audiences were seeing something new. The "problem pictures," for all their flaws, were "worth seeing," said Ellison. With Black audiences, "when the action goes phony one will hear derisive laughter," but with white audiences, Ellison witnessed "the profuse flow of tears and the sighs of profound emotional catharsis heard on all sides. It is as though there were some deep relief to be gained merely from seeing these subjects projected upon the screen."

Seen today, the once-shocking film has a reassuring fairy-tale look. De Rochemont filmed this "drama of real life" on location in Portsmouth, New Hampshire, and in Kittery and Kennebunkport, Maine, using locals as extras. The scenes of a New England now seventy years gone give the film a fable-like quality, enhanced by the black-and-white photography (as if black and white possessed some extra clarity). The old Yankees, the avenue of elms framing the white church steeple, the old house interiors elegant in their simplicity, give us a landscape of virtue, the locus of the American conscience. If anyone will do right, we are assured, it is New Englanders. When the family's secret comes out, some people whisper and turn away. No one attacks them. There are no scenes of angry crowds or burning crosses.

In the end, all are in the House of the Lord, hat-in-hand, kneeling on Sunday, ready for a Norman Rockwell portrait. The reverend— played by a real reverend—preaches Christian brotherhood and leads the singing of poet James Russell Lowell's hymn, "Once to every man and nation, comes the moment to decide." As the choir files out of the church, a man standing in the pew in front of the doctor turns to shake his hand. He's their neighbor; they will stand by him. The doctor keeps his job; the family stays.

In one scene, when the town is buzzing with gossip, the doctor's daughter runs into her boyfriend. "There's an awful rumor going around town about you folks," he says. "They were saying your folks are colored."

She replies, "Are they saying bad things about us?"

In an era of mammies and Uncle Toms, dialogue like this was like a clearing in the forest.

After their story was out, were they saying bad things about the Johnstons? The national press wanted to know. "The Johnstons, a leading family in Keene, N. H., last spring let the world know that they were Negroes. The reaction? There was none," reported *Look* magazine. All was well, *Look* assured readers. Daughter Anne, shown playing cards encircled by white friends, is still the "most popular girl in her high school class," and the family "is one of the most socially accepted and prosperous in the town."

"Nothing significant happened. Nothing, except that we continued to live as equals in a town which wears its democracy like a shining shield," Albert told *Ebony* five years after their story was known. He was proud of his neighbors. "They are strong and unyielding, like the granite foothills surrounding our little city. They respect human rights and are willing to give a man a break regardless of his color. Maybe the world outside feels that we live here like flowers in a florist's hothouse, but this is not the truth. We are a part of Keene, part of the pulse, and the soul of this city."

The Johnstons' white neighbors were treated as heroes in these stories for what they didn't do. They didn't form a mob to attack the family—mob violence was the unstated comparison. The year *Reader's Digest* published *Lost Boundaries*, 1947, Sinclair Lewis's bestselling novel, *Kingsblood Royal*, told a story of a white family who discovered they had a Black ancestor. It did not end well.

In the novel, Neil Kingsblood is a war hero, a bank cashier who lives in a whites-only neighborhood of his Minnesota town. Believing that he is related to British royalty, he researches his genealogy only to come across an unexpected ancestor, a "full blooded Negro," a frontier trader married to a Chippewa Indian. Neil is no longer white. Blacks, he believed, were ignorant and lazy. He had to face the "astonishing collapse of everything that had been Neil Kingsblood." He was not who he thought he was. When he lets his discovery be known, he loses his bank job. Worse things follow. A mob surrounds his house, demanding that he move. They shoot, grazing his wife, and in reply Neil Kingsblood takes up his shotgun and fires into the crowd. The police restore order—by arresting Neil and his wife. Sinclair Lewis based his novel on a real story.

"Take the hatred out of *Kingsblood Royal* and little is left; there is no hatred in *Lost Boundaries*," said the *Keene Sentinel* at the movie's premiere in town.

The Johnstons' story was not *Kingsblood Royal*. And yet.

Dr. Johnston lost his job at the hospital. A year after praising his neighbors, he was fired.

∽

When Donald Johnston's daughter was born, the city clerk called him at home to fill out the birth certificate:

"What will the girl be, white or colored?"

"White," Donald answered.

Her mother is white, his birth certificate said he was white, "so wouldn't it look odd for our child to be called colored?" Eventually, he said, his daughter "will have to know about the color thing . . . but we don't know yet how or when to tell her. It is a big problem."

There were still boundaries for the Johnstons in Keene. The question of their race hovered in the background, but the family was committed to telling a positive story. While the magazine reports are blissfully free of hate, another story shows through, comments slipping out, as if the community were trying to hold its breath around the Johnstons. "My high school friends never say anything to embarrass me," said Anne. "Of course, now and then there is a slip. If someone is passing around a pack of cigarettes and they accidently miss someone, that person may say, before he thinks, 'What's the matter, am I colored?' Then there is a silence."

Another time Anne was with her friends discussing the news, a lynching down south. One boy, the class valedictorian, said "of course Negroes are okay, but keep them in their place." Anne argued with the boy. Sure, he replied, some were intelligent, but "most of them were just cotton pickers." This is what Albert Jr. had heard when he hitchhiked across the country: "Yes, the Negro deserves an opportunity. I know of many intelligent, hard-working Negroes. But we think they must keep their place."

And this was the message the hospital delivered to Dr. Johnston by firing him. The president of the hospital's board insisted that it had nothing to do with his race. They said it was about economics. Radiology was profitable, supporting money-losing departments. With the hospital facing a deficit, the board wanted to charge more for X-rays. Dr. Johnston thought this was unfair to patients. They also wanted to cut the commission he received for the X-rays. He called in a lawyer to negotiate a contract following the guidelines of the American College of Radiology, which supported him in this dispute. The board rejected that offer and refused to negotiate. He had built up the Radiology Department's income four-fold, and the board was pleased with his work—when he was white. One day soon after the *Reader's Digest* story was out, he was accidently introduced to his intended replacement, who, it turned out, would be paid more than him. To protect himself, Dr. Johnston started a private practice. The board held that against him, too.

That was the rationale. The motivation was clear to the Johnstons. "We know we are fighting prejudice," Thyra told Louis de Rochemont. They were facing the "malicious jealousy" of a "small click." Dr. Johnston had confronted the trustee who was trying to oust him, and "he had the nerve to practically admit it was a color issue," said Thyra. "They will stoop to any means to get him out."

"They have been picking on me ever since my story came out," Dr. Johnston told *Jet* magazine. "Somebody began knifing me," he said. After more than five years of acrimony, he was fired in 1953.

Decades later, no one would talk about why the hospital fired him. It was an "unpleasant time around here," said one doctor who counted himself as a friend. He refused to say much else. "There were no racial overtones. That was to produce a movie," he said with annoyance. Another doctor evaded all questions, saying, "I've already said more than I should."

His firing was like a letter his son Donald had received from a close friend, a girl from a prominent Yankee family. The two had grown up together. She liked him and still wanted to see him, she wrote, but she was forbidden. Her father didn't approve of Blacks (or Jews or Catholics).

Battling to keep his job—a job he was good at—had left Albert in a somber mood. "Americans in general do not want to do anything about race prejudice. They have been pampering their nasty little prejudices for years," he said. He thought there was more prejudice than in his youth. He began giving lectures for the NAACP around the country. "Nature does not give talents according to color, and the Lord only knows how many Edisons or Einsteins have spent their life mopping floors because of the lack of opportunity to develop latent talents," he said in one speech.

Years of passing had fed his anger. He had endured southern doctors at medical conventions telling him what was wrong with Negroes. "'Johnston, you just don't know the problem. Negroes don't have the brains, or any sense of moral values like you and I have. You have to treat 'em like that.' And I have to sit there silent and take it—feeling like a traitor."

This was another cost that passing exacted, one familiar to many Blacks, including Malcolm X, who said, "I will tell you that, without any question, the most bitter anti-white diatribes that I have ever heard have come from 'passing' Negroes, living as whites, among whites, exposed every day to what white people say among themselves regarding Negroes—things that a recognized Negro never would hear. Why, if there was a racial showdown, these Negroes 'passing' within white circles would become the Black side's most valuable 'spy' and ally."

In one of his NAACP speeches in the 1950s, Albert said: "The rising deep seated resentment of the Negro toward his treatment by many of his countrymen, and especially by his government, will sooner or later disrupt the harmony of this nation." This was not something the jovial Baron spinning tales at Harvard would have said, or what the country doctor would have said living on the hill in Gorham, president of everything, hosting the best parties of the year.

He practiced another thirteen years in Keene, serving nearby hospitals. In 1966 Albert and Thyra moved to Hawaii. The races are already mixing there, Thyra said. The doctor had intended to retire, but when he arrived on Kauai, he found out there was no radiologist on the island, so he sent for his equipment and practiced for another fifteen years. The Johnstons were happy in Hawaii. Two sons, Albert Jr. and the youngest, Paul, moved to Honolulu to be closer to their parents. Thyra and Albert took up hobbies; she painted and he enjoyed photography, which he had first learned for his medical lectures. They took three trips around the world, including an African safari. "The years have been good to Dr. and Mrs. Johnston," *Jet* reported in 1969. "He is president of the medical society in his new hometown of

Kuawaii. Still in good health, he enjoys his work at the hospital, his dips in his backyard swimming pool and the exchange trips with his children and grandchildren."

IV. And Yet

Dr. Johnston died at age eighty-seven in 1988. His body was returned to be buried in Keene. Johnstons arrived from all over, and after the funeral some relatives began to look for a copy of that film they'd heard about, the one about their family. They had never seen it. One of the granddaughters called Keene's library, which put her in touch with someone who might have a copy, a film professor at Keene State College, Larry Benaquist. He had been showing *Lost Boundaries* to his students, and he had just purchased a copy. He drove down to Massachusetts where the family had gathered, and set up his projector and a screen. Thyra, sitting on the other side of the projector, would tap him on the knee, to whisper, "That's exactly how it happened in real life." When the film was over, one granddaughter was sobbing, saying, "I don't know who I am." She grew up in a small New Hampshire town. When they were discussing Blacks, the teacher said, "We have one here. Would you stand up so we can look at you?"

After that showing, Benaquist organized a big reunion at the college. Forty years after *Lost Boundaries* was first shown in Keene, the Johnstons returned, along with some of the actors, including Mel Ferrer, Susan Douglas, Carleton Carpenter, William Greaves, many extras, some of the production staff, and Louis de Rochemont's widow, Virginia, who wrote the screenplay.

At the reunion, a crowded auditorium rose to give the Johnston family—Thyra, her children, grandchildren, and great grandchildren—a standing ovation. Albert Jr. stood with tears in his eyes. A proclamation from the governor was read, saying that state recognition was "long overdue for this great family." Dr. Johnston, said the proclamation, was a "true patriot."

After a few speeches and the film, a long line of Thyra's friends formed, just spontaneously. One by one they stood and embraced her.

Consenting to tell their story, she said, had been one of the "anxious episodes in our life, not knowing whether Dr. Johnston or I should rejoice or cry when the story first appeared in print in *Reader's Digest*. We were very hesitant about some of the first reactions of some of the townspeople. I think the film helped soften the edges." For two years, the Johnstons had lived in limbo, not really knowing what many of their neighbors thought. "Believe me, we were relieved of most of our anxiety *after* the picture was shown."

But it was not until the reunion forty years later that Thyra would be relieved of all her doubt. She had always felt that they left town under a cloud. "It warmed my heart to see so many friends and patients of Dr. Johnston who came from far and near to pay tribute to their doctor. It was not until that memorable fortieth celebration evening before the showing of the picture that *I* was *sure* that we had made the right decision."

In a documentary about the reunion shown on New Hampshire Public Television, Thyra sat facing the camera with Alice Andrews, who was the Johnstons' maid. Alice sat holding Thyra's hand. "They were asking why I was working for niggers," said Alice, who is white. "I never told her that because I didn't want to hurt her feelings."

Thyra said, "She has heard these things, but I have never heard them."

Thyra Johnston speaks of forgiveness. "We never want to hurt Keene. And that's why we don't like to say there was any race prejudice. There's still a lot of pressure—don't let anybody tell you there isn't. But New Hampshire is a beautiful place," she said, and the people are good. "Lots of times people do feel sorry afterwards. So if they have said anything or tried to do anything, I'm quite forgiving. And I think that's the way it should be."

V. Slip the Yoke

In Allyson Hobb's history of passing, *A Chosen Exile*, she tells a story of trading places, of a reversal of fortune. Black Matt, a slave trader in Louisiana in the 1850s, is trying to sell Sam, a light-skinned African, as a manservant. Black Matt dresses Sam in a fine coat and boots, whereupon Sam takes the opportunity to "slip the yoke" and sell his dark-skinned master into slavery. This is a trickster's fable, a wish, not an actuality, a longed-for turnabout. Sweet, swift justice. Sam pocketed his profit and sailed for Europe, never to be heard from again. But our responsibility to face the entire bitter history of slavery and racism, America's original sin, doesn't end this way. We don't get "to skip ahead to the finish line of racial harmony," as writer Ijeoma Oluo says. We don't get to sail away like Sam, who was free at last, free at last, thank God almighty, free at last.

FORTY ACRES AND A MULE

The Promised Land Denied

I. "You Are Our Moses!"—1864

In "the fourth year of the rebellion," just weeks before election day, a correspondent from the *Cincinnati Gazette* was in Nashville, "the proud city of the slaveholders," for a nighttime campaign rally. Abraham Lincoln was running for a second term, this time with the military governor of Tennessee, Andrew Johnson, a Democrat and a slave owner until just a few months prior. That night, Johnson addressed a crowd of the recently freed, a gathering who could not vote. His speech "was one of the most remarkable to which it was ever my fortune to listen," said the reporter. As he made his way across the city, the reporter heard the "cheers and shouts" of the "vast crowd" gathered in the "ruddy glow" of torchlight, packed in tight before Johnson.

"Colored Men of Nashville," Johnson began, "I, too, without reference to the president or any other person, have a proclamation to make; and, standing here upon the steps of the capitol, with the past history of the State to witness, the present condition to guide, and its future to encourage me, I, Andrew Johnson, do hereby proclaim freedom, full, broad, and unconditional, to every man in Tennessee!"

Lincoln's Emancipation Proclamation, two year earlier, had left out Tennessee at Johnson's insistence. The border state would wait until 1865 to outlaw slavery.

"With breathless attention those sons of bondage hung upon each syllable; each individual seemed carved in stone until the last word

HOWARD MANSFIELD

of the grand climax was reached; and then the scene which followed beggars all description. One simultaneous roar of approval and delight burst from three thousand throats. Flags, banners, torches . . . were waved wildly over the throng, or flung aloft in the ecstasy of joy. Drums, fifes, and trumpets added to the uproar," said the reporter. "It was one of those moments when the speaker seems inspired, and when his audience, catching the inspiration, rises to his level and becomes one with him."

Johnson attacked some of the wealthiest men in Tennessee by name, calling them a "corrupt" and "damnable aristocracy." He had risen from poverty and blamed the plantation owners for the war. "I say if their immense plantations were divided up and parceled out amongst a number of free, industrious, and honest farmers, it would give more good citizens to the commonwealth, increase the wages of our mechanics, enrich the markets of our city, enliven all the arteries of trade, improve society, and conduce to the greatness and glory of the state.

"I wish to see secured to every man, rich or poor, the fruits of his honest industry, effort, or toil. I want each man to feel that what he has gained by his own skill, or talent, or exertion, is rightfully his, and his alone.

"Looking at this vast crowd of colored people," Johnson continued, "and reflecting through what a storm of persecution and obloquy they are compelled to pass, I am almost induced to wish that, as in the days of old, a Moses might arise who should lead them safely to their promised land of freedom and happiness."

"You are our Moses!" several people shouted. The crowd repeated "You are our Moses!" and cheered.

"God no doubt has prepared somewhere an instrument for the great work he designs to perform in behalf of this outraged people, and in due time your leader will come forth," said Johnson. "Your Moses will be revealed to you."

"We want no Moses but you!" the crowd shouted.

"Well, then," Johnson replied, "humble and unworthy as I am, if no other better shall be found, I will indeed be your Moses, and lead you through the Red Sea of war and bondage to a fairer future of liberty and peace. . . . I mean to stay and fight this great battle of truth and justice to a triumphant end."

"It is impossible to describe the enthusiasm which followed these words," wrote the reporter. People rejoiced; some cried. "The great throng moved and swayed back and forth in the intensity of emotion, and shout after shout rent the air."

But Andrew Johnson was no Moses. He had contempt for Blacks. In a time of publicly proclaimed racism, his hatred stood out. His speech that night in Nashville has long puzzled historians. It's the point on the graph that doesn't join with the other points, an outlier. Some have thought he was drunk. None of this mattered until Lincoln was assassinated in April 1865.

For one night, Johnson played at being a prophet. In a country at war, where four million Blacks had been enslaved by eight million whites in the South, the story of Moses and Exodus was close at hand. The Promised Land wasn't just a Bible story.

Johnson's speech inspired a song that was published in 1866:

Where is our Moses that once was to be
To lead us afar thro' the deep Red Sea? . . .
Hear us Oh Moses! From once made a vow
To lead us afar, where, oh where is he now?

II. The Accidental Moses—1865

When General William Tecumseh Sherman's army of sixty thousand marched to the sea after burning Atlanta, inflicting total war on Georgia, they were trailed by a growing number escaping slavery, perhaps as many as nineteen thousand men, women, and children, "a dark human cloud that hung like remorse on the rear of those swift columns," said the scholar and activist W. E. B. Dubois. The Union army was their only refuge. Sherman wanted nothing to do with these "camp followers." He wanted to keep his army moving "to whip the rebels, to humble their pride, to follow them to their inmost recesses, and make them fear and dread us." He would cut the Confederacy in half.

Sherman's army captured Savannah just before Christmas. "When the morning light of the 22nd of December, 1864, broke in upon us, the streets of our city were thronged in every part with the victorious army of liberty," recalled the Rev. James M. Simms of the First African Baptist Church. "Every . . . military movement told us that they had come for our deliverance, and were able to secure it to us, and the cry went around the city from house to house among our race of people, 'Glory be to God, we are free!'" Reverend Simms offered a hymn of thanksgiving:

> Shout the glad tidings o'er Egypt's dark sea
> Jehovah has triumphed, his people are free!

The enslaved had prayed for the Union army. Susie King Taylor, who was born into slavery, recalled, "I wanted to see these wonderful 'Yankees' so much, as I heard my parents say the Yankee was going to set all the slaves free. Oh, how those people prayed for freedom!" One night her grandmother had gone to a church meeting outside the city, where "they were fervently singing this old hymn":

> Yes, we all shall be free,
> Yes, we all shall be free . . .
> When the Lord shall appear

The police arrived to arrest everyone there, saying they were plotting to escape. Singing about the Lord, the police said, was just a code word to use in place of "Yankee."

But the Union army could be cruel, sometimes confiscating what little the freed slaves had. They had burned a Black church in Atlanta. At a creek crossing twenty miles north of Savannah, one of Sherman's generals had pulled up a pontoon bridge before the hundreds of freed old men, women, and children who were following his troops could cross. The able-bodied men had been sent forward to repair roads.

Waiting for the army to pass first, as they'd been ordered, with the Confederate cavalry closing in, they panicked when the bridge was removed and "rushed by the hundreds" into the December-cold, roiling water, "and many were drowned before our eyes," said a colonel. It was "a scene the like of which I pray my eyes may never see again." Those who stayed ashore were killed by the Confederates or returned to slavery. This incident became a scandal in the North. Sherman dismissed it as "a cock-and-bull story." He stood by his general. The Yankees brought their prejudices south with them.

Sherman was a white supremacist. He thought that no Black was the equal of a white man—he "is not a white man, and all the Psalm singing on earth won't make him so," Sherman said. He did not want Blacks in his army; he did not trust them. He ignored Lincoln's orders to recruit Black soldiers. When the army's adjutant general addressed Sherman's men, telling them they had to learn to fight alongside Blacks, Sherman immediately told his troops that he hoped the policy could be revised so Black men would not be "brigaded with white men." He contradicted army policy, issuing his own order saying that any officer recruiting Black men would be arrested. Black recruitment "is the height of folly," he wrote to the general-in-chief who was in charge of the Union army. Lincoln finally wrote to remind him that recruiting Blacks was the law, and "being a law, it must be treated by all of us." Lincoln asked for his general's "hearty cooperation." Sherman ignored the president. "I am honest in my belief that it is not fair to our men to count Negroes as equals," he said, adding that a Negro was "as good as a white man to stop a bullet," but "a sand bag is better."

His racism and the mayhem at the creek crossing brought Secretary of War Edwin M. Stanton to Savannah to talk things over. He arrived with a regiment of Black troops to join Sherman's army. Sherman disarmed the soldiers and gave them shovels. His men attacked the newcomers, killing at least three. Sherman's troops remained all-white until the war's end, and this in an army where 10 percent of the soldiers were black.

Stanton, an abolitionist long opposed to slavery, wanted to meet some freedmen to hear from them directly. He asked Sherman to find the community's Black leaders or, as Sherman said, "the most intelligent of the Negroes."

Sherman and Stanton met twenty men at the house the general had taken as his headquarters. They were primarily Baptist and Methodist ministers, ranging in age from twenty-six to seventy-two years old. Five of the twenty were freeborn, and six others had won their freedom before the war. In this they were not a representative group: in 1860 only 5 percent of Blacks in America were free. Several of them would become leaders during the post-war Reconstruction era. "These were men of talent, ambition, and standing, fully prepared for the challenges of freedom," says historian Eric Foner.

The group chose Garrison Frazier, a Baptist minister, age sixty-seven, as their spokesman for what became known as the Savannah Colloquy. Eight years before, Frazier had been enslaved. He bought freedom for himself and his wife, paying $1,000 in gold and silver. The secretary of war asked twelve questions. Among his questions and Frazier's answers:

State what you understand by slavery and the freedom that was to be given by the President's proclamation.

"Slavery is, receiving by irresistible power the work of another man, and not by his consent. The freedom, as I understand it, promised by the proclamation, is taking us from under the yoke of bondage, and placing us where we could reap the fruit of our own labor, take care of ourselves and assist the Government in maintaining our freedom."

State in what manner you think you can take care of yourselves, and how can you best assist the Government in maintaining your freedom.

"The way we can best take care of ourselves is to have land, and turn it and till it by our own labor . . . and we can soon maintain ourselves and have something to spare. . . . We want to be placed on land until we are able to buy it and make it our own."

State in what manner you would rather live—whether scattered among the whites or in colonies by yourselves.

Frazier answered for himself: "I would prefer to live by ourselves, for there is a prejudice against us in the South that will take years to get over; but I do not know that I can answer for my brethren." All but one of the other nineteen present, questioned individually, agreed.

For the last question, Stanton asked Sherman to leave the room. Sherman thought it a "strange" request. After all, he had "commanded one hundred thousand men in battle" and "had just brought tens of thousands of freedmen to a place of security," but he did as he was asked.

State what is the feeling of the colored people in regard to General Sherman; and how far do they regard his sentiments and actions as friendly to their rights and interests, or otherwise?

"We looked upon General Sherman prior to his arrival as a man in the Providence of God specially set apart to accomplish this work, and we unanimously feel inexpressible gratitude to him, looking upon him as a man that should be honored for the faithful performance of his duty. Some of us called upon him immediately upon his arrival, and it is probable he would not meet the secretary with more courtesy than he met us. His conduct and deportment toward us characterized him as a friend and a gentleman. We have confidence in General Sherman, and think that what concerns us could not be under better hands."

Stanton sent his transcript of the meeting to his friend Henry Ward Beecher, the famous abolitionist minister of New York's Plymouth Church. "For the first time in the history of this nation, the representatives of the government had gone to these poor debased people to ask them what they wanted for themselves," Stanton said. Beecher read the transcript from his pulpit.

∼

Four days after the meeting, on January 16, 1865, Sherman issued Special Field Order 15. Stanton had reviewed the order, one of the boldest moves of the war. It set aside a broad swath of land for freedmen, reaching from Charleston, South Carolina, into Florida:

"The islands from Charleston south, the abandoned rice-fields along the rivers for thirty miles back from the sea, and the country bordering the St. John's River, Florida, are reserved and set apart for the settlement of the Negroes now made free by the acts of war and the proclamation of the President of the United States.

"On the islands, and in the settlements hereafter to be established, no white person whatever, unless military officers and soldiers detailed for duty, will be permitted to reside; and the sole and exclusive management of affairs will be left to the freed people themselves, subject only to the United States military authority, and the acts of Congress."

The order continued, saying that "each family shall have a plot of not more than forty acres of tillable ground" and the protection of the military "until such time as they can protect themselves, or until Congress shall regulate their title." The army would, if requested, also make available "one or more of the captured steamers to ply between the settlements and . . . commercial points" so the freedmen could obtain supplies and "sell the products of their land and labor." The order also encouraged enlistment, promising the enlistee's family a homestead and a bounty to be used to buy "agricultural implements, seed, tools, boats, clothing, and other articles necessary for their livelihood."

Brigadier General Rufus Saxton was appointed under the order to oversee parceling out the land. Saxton had won the military's highest decoration, the Medal of Honor, for his defense of Harper's Ferry in 1862. He was a dedicated abolitionist who had recruited the first regiments of Black soldiers. Three years before the field order he had proposed that land be set aside for the freedmen. Saxton had seen the freedmen succeed when he was in charge of what was called the Port Royal Experiment—fifteen thousand freedmen farming captured plantations. He had gathered them to read the Emancipation

Proclamation. "It is your duty to carry this good news to your brethren who are still in slavery," he said. "Let all your voices, like merry bells, join loud and clear in the grand chorus of liberty – 'We are free, we are free.'" He also urged them to petition Congress for the right to vote. Sherman saw the land grants as an expedient way to clear the camp followers from his army. He was only accidently a reformer. For Saxton, the promise was a mandate.

Special Field Order 15 became known as "forty acres and a mule," but mules were not in the official order. They were an afterthought. Sherman's men had seized many more mules and horses than his army needed. He gave the "partially broken down" animals to Saxton to loan to the freedmen setting up their farms.

In six months, by early June, Saxton had settled forty thousand people on four hundred thousand acres of "Sherman Land."

III. The Apprentice Moses—1865

Exodus, it has been said, is a never-ending story. The flight from Egypt was not a clean escape, but a perilous journey. And so it was for the freedmen. Sherman Land was not the Promised Land but a fraught and fractured beginning. Special Field Order 15 was an improvisation, an attempt to answer questions most Americans weren't ready to ask: How do you end 250 years of slavery? And what is owed to those you have enslaved?

Congress searched for a more extensive answer, establishing the Freedmen's Bureau in 1865. Originally proposed as the Bureau of Emancipation, it passed the House by just two votes. The Senate amended the bill, making changes the House refused. The next year it was hastily rewritten and passed. One Kentucky senator called it "a bill to promote strife and conflict between the white and black races . . . by a grant of unconstitutional powers." An Iowa senator objected to any group getting special treatment under the law. "If they are free men, why not let them stand as free men?" he asked. Lincoln signed the bill eleven days before he was murdered.

The new bureau was assigned an incredibly broad mandate: set up a free market for workers; start schools where there had been none; supply temporary shelter, clothing, and food for the "destitute and suffering," the aged, ill, and insane (white as well as Black); settle disputes between the races and among the freedmen; insure that Blacks received equal justice from state and local governments; and allocate 850,000 acres of seized and abandoned land to the freedmen. The bill establishing the bureau did not mention Sherman's order. It said that freedmen could rent forty acres for three years with an option to buy.

The bureau would have to be "diplomat, marriage counselor, educator, supervisor of labor contracts, sheriff, judge, and jury," said historian Foner. The federal government had never before claimed such an active role in defining and protecting the rights of citizens. It wasn't just that Congress was asking a lot of the government, it was asking for a social service agency that was a half-century ahead of its time, something that would have to wait until Franklin Delano Roosevelt's New Deal took on the Great Depression. The Freedmen's Bureau had no budget. It was supposed to support itself by renting out the land it controlled. The bureau was part of the War Department and staffed by the army. At its peak, nine hundred officers were expected to cover the South. The bureau was also temporary; it would expire in a year.

To lead the bureau, Stanton appointed a respected general, Oliver Otis Howard, the choice of the late president. Howard had lost his right arm at the Battle of Fair Oaks early in the war, in 1862. His arm was amputated between the elbow and the shoulder. He returned to fight three months later at Antietam, and the next year at Gettysburg. On Sherman's March to the Sea, Howard commanded the army of the Tennessee, the right wing of the attack. After this he was posted at Beaufort, South Carolina, where he was impressed with the Port Royal Experiment. He had considered himself an abolitionist long before the war, a view that was unpopular among many of his southern classmates at West Point.

The Christian General, as he was known, had a religious conversion when he came forward to be saved at a Methodist revival, determined to be "on the side of those who were trying to do God's will." "I trembled like a leaf, but my head was clear & I didn't shed tears like the rest," he said. But later, alone, praying, "the fullness of the glow of happiness came into my heart," he wrote to his wife. "The choking sensation was gone & for once I enjoyed present happiness. Oh! how sweet & delightful it seemed. . . . I didn't sleep much, I was too happy." He was saved. "There is now a new well spring within me, a joy, a peace & a trusting spirit." He had "something to live for, a great work to do." He was twenty-six years old. He seriously considered becoming a minister. He taught Sunday school, didn't drink, smoke, swear, or play cards, and made the men under his command attend Sunday Bible school. Taking his first command as a colonel, he greeted his men with a sermon on the Ten Commandments.

His opposition to slavery grew during the war but was contained by his fidelity to the army rulebook. Early in the war, a mother and her ten-year-old son came to the camp he was commanding in Virginia and begged for their freedom. At that date he was "under the most stringent orders not to harbor any slave property." She was followed into camp by her owner, "a poorly clad white woman," demanding her "property" and an armed escort.

The fleeing woman "kept pressing her child to her breast and with her large eyes filled with tears continued to look toward me, repeating: 'Oh! my child, my child!'" Howard recalled. She "said she would drown herself before she would go back," said his brother, Charles, who was his aide.

At first Howard thought he would have to return the woman to slavery. Those were his orders, but his "heart rebelled." He would not "use bayonets to drive a poor girl and her child into bondage." He told the slave owner to come back tomorrow; he had to check with headquarters. On her return, he said she could take her "property," but there would be no armed guard, knowing that would stop her. He had "reluctantly complied with the letter of the law." He was a principled compromiser—this was the line he walked; this was the contradiction that was to guide and hinder him. That night, the woman and her child escaped to freedom.

Some northerners wanted the rebels punished. Howard was forgiving—too much so, his critics said. "We must seek courage and strength from on high so as to lay aside all malice, all purposes of revenge, and put on a broad, living charity, no less than love to God and love to his children," he said.

His new nine-to-five job was to bring freedom, equality, respect, and a free market to a region of slavery. "I fear you have Hercules' task," his old friend Sherman told him, predicting he would be unable "to fill one tenth part of the expectation" for the bureau. He went at his job with a kind of dogged, rigid-backed moralism: We'll rise and do right every day, and the world will see this rightness and fall in line. "The negroes must be employed, instructed, cloaked, and fed, borne with and kindly treated as well as emancipated," he wrote to his wife. "God in his wise providence will hold us to it at the north and at the south."

There is a Sunday school teacher's insistence behind the entire bureau. In his first official communication detailing the bureau's operation, he called for "simple good faith, for which we hope on all hands for those concerned in the passing away of slavery" to help the bureau aid the freedmen and "promote the general welfare."

On his first day, Stanton handed the one-armed veteran a "large, oblong bushel basket heaped with letters and documents," saying with a smile, "Here, general, here's your bureau!" The Freedmen's Bureau was another improvisation.

IV. "This Is a Country for White Men"—1865 (and Earlier and Later)

The Freedmen's Bureau hadn't even begun when it ran into Andrew Johnson. During the first eight months after the war, Congress was out of session, leaving Johnson to act without restraint. The new president worked to reunite North and South as he wished. "This is a country for white men and by God, as long as I am president, it shall be a government for white men," he said. "Of all the dangers which our nation has yet encountered, none are equal to those which must result from the success of the effort . . . to Africanize the half of our country," he said in one of his more temperate statements on race. Blacks, he believed, had less "capacity for government than any other race. . . . Whenever they have been left to their own devices they have shown a constant tendency to lapse into barbarism." The Moses of that night in Nashville was forgotten.

The president and the southern white planters hated the Freedmen's Bureau. Before he was vice president, Johnson had said the plantation owners were traitors who must be brought to justice, their plantations divided among the workingmen, but now he was their friend in the White House. Working with Johnson, the southerners defeated land reform, fighting to get back every acre granted to freedmen. They gutted the bureau, reducing its mission until it was managing their farm labor, enforcing their contracts, in some places rounding up freedmen in the city to go pick cotton, and requiring passes for travel, just like the old "slave masters." "They are, in fact, the planter's guards and nothing else," said the *New Orleans Tribune*.

The bureau forced freedmen to sign one-year contracts in January with wages to be held until the crops were in, essentially making the farmhands underwrite the planting season. Delayed pay was a loan from those with the least to those with the most. Idle whites were not tied to annual contracts. "If you call this freedom, what do you call slavery?" asked one Black Union veteran. The bureau tried to stand "forth between the two classes," said Howard, negotiating for fair pay, but wages varied widely, and there were sometimes bloody clashes with former slave owners shooting the new freedmen. The old slave masters wanted contract labor to be slavery by another name. Blacks were "free, but free only to labor," they said. The bureau was left to enforce an oxymoron, a "compulsory system of free labor," said

Foner. It was a system Howard endorsed. (He even had a political organizer, one of the nation's first Black lawyers, arrested for speaking against the contracts.) He believed that contract labor would stabilize the South within five years so his bureau could withdraw. Contracts would benefit the former slavers and the enslaved. Hard work would build "manly individualism and self-reliance," he believed, purifying and strengthening the "emancipated . . . just as the children of Israel were by the experiences they encountered on passing from Egypt to the Promised Land."

Education was the bureau's greatest success. Prior to the war, anyone caught teaching Blacks or mulattos in the slave states would be fined, whipped, or imprisoned. The bureau sent a legion of New England schoolmarms south to teach where it was once forbidden. Almost two-thirds of Blacks lived in counties with at least one bureau school.

At a more basic level, the bureau acted effectively—for a time, providing over 13 million rations, two-thirds to Blacks, in the first fifteen months after the war. (A ration was enough corn meal, flour, and sugar to feed a person for a week.) Howard abruptly cut off rations in the fall of 1866. He was constantly fighting critics who said the bureau was encouraging "idleness" and "dependency," but with the harvest lost to drought, flooding, and a worm infestation, he relented, offering some rations. Many freedmen were facing starvation. The southern states refused to feed them. "Not a *dam bite* will I give them. I would choose *hell* first," said an overseer of the poor in Virginia.

No matter what it did, the Freedmen's Bureau stood across a great divide from southern whites. "The whole thought seems to be, how can we white men maintain our authority over these black men?" said Howard. "How can we keep them from renting and owning land; how hinder them from suits and testimony against us? How can we restrain them from rising in the social scale; how prevent their individuality from cropping out; their holding meetings; their bearing arms; how prevent them from having a voice in making or executing the laws? . . . They heartily disbelieve in freedom for the Negro."

Howard's bureau believed in equality before the law. It ran its own courts and tried to convince the South to have fair courts, but any gain for Blacks in freedom and equality was seen by whites as a loss. Freedom in this view was a zero-sum game. "The basic problem," said the bureau's Mississippi director, "is that whites could not conceive of the Negro having any rights at all. . . . They still have an ingrained feeling that the black people at large belong to the whites at large."

"Contemplating the struggle actually going on," said Howard, "the heart is often balanced between hope and fear."

"Of all that most Americans wanted, this freeing of slaves was the last," said W. E. B. Dubois in his groundbreaking history of the Reconstruction era. "Everything black was hideous. Everything Negroes did was wrong. If they fought for freedom, they were beasts; if they did not fight, they were born slaves. If they cowered on the plantations, they loved slavery; if they ran away, they were lazy loafers. If they sang, they were silly; if they scowled, they were impudent."

Throughout the South, they were relentlessly attacked and killed. The president did nothing to stop this; there were no consequences for vigilantes. Arsonists attacked the bureau's schools almost nightly. They chased freedmen out of town. Delegates to Black political conventions returned home to find only "ash and cinders." Africans were still enslaved in Nashville almost a year after the end of the war. Some plantation owners were waiting for slavery to resume. The bureau had a hard time freeing them.

"Southern whites are quite indignant if they are not treated with the same deference" as before, said a bureau agent. In South Carolina, a minister shot a freedman "thru the heart" after he objected to a Black being thrown out of church. The bureau recorded the "reasons" for some of the one thousand murders of Blacks by whites in Texas over three years: one man "did not remove his hat," a woman "refused to call him master," still another was killed just to "thin out" the Black population, and another was gunned down just to see him "kick." Freedmen in Texas reported seeing bodies floating downriver. In Mississippi, attackers cut the throat of a "man known to speak his mind" and disemboweled him as his wife was forced to watch. Settlements were burned in Arkansas. Witnesses found twenty-four men, women, and children hanging from the trees near Pine Bluff. (Before the war there was no lynching; the enslaved were valuable property.) In parts of Tennessee, a hate group known as the Regulators were "riding about, whipping, maiming, and killing all Negroes who do not obey the orders of their former masters, just as if slavery existed."

Blacks holding political office faced violence daily. They lived in fear. The goal is to kill the leaders, said a representative to Florida's constitutional convention who was forced to leave the county. Whites who sold or rented land to freedmen were beaten and whipped and their farm buildings set afire. In Florida and elsewhere, the Ku Klux Klan killed livestock owned by Blacks so they could not be economically independent. The Klan's three-year-long "reign of terror" in the Florida panhandle killed 150, including a Jewish merchant who was guilty of treating Blacks fairly. "If a white man kills a colored man in any of the counties of this state you cannot convict him," regretted one Florida sheriff. Florida's governor, appointed by Johnson, made the freedmen's status clear: "You must not think because you are as free as white people, that you are their equal, because you are not."

In addition to targeted killings, there were riots. In a Memphis riot lasting three days, forty-six Blacks were killed and hundreds were injured. A white mob, led by a city official "who urged the wholesale slaughter of blacks," swarmed a Black neighborhood. The mob burned three Black churches, eight schools (five belonging to the Freedmen's Bureau), and fifty houses. In some burning houses, the family's escape was stopped by armed men. "All crimes imaginable were committed from simple larceny to rape and murder. Several women and children were shot in bed," said the bureau's report. "Although many of the perpetrators are known, no arrests have been made." In New Orleans, police attacked a Black political meeting, killing forty-seven Black delegates and three white delegates and wounding one hundred thirty-six. This violence foreshadowed the election year carnage in 1868, when a thousand Blacks and whites were killed in Louisiana, six hundred in Kentucky, and dozens more elsewhere.

Congressman Robert Smalls, who had escaped from slavery, said that by the time he left office in March 1887, fifty-three thousand Blacks had been murdered, mostly in the South. In addition, smallpox ravaged the freedmen. One-quarter of their population died from this and other illnesses.

The first summer after the war, Johnson sent Carl Schurz, a journalist, to investigate conditions in the South. Schurz reported back to the president throughout his three-month tour, later writing:

"I saw in various hospitals Negroes, women as well as men, whose ears had been cut off or whose bodies were slashed with knives or bruised with whips, or bludgeons, or punctured with shot wounds. Dead Negroes were found in considerable number in the country roads or on the fields, shot to death, or strung upon the limbs of trees. In many districts the colored people were in a panic of fright, and the whites in a state of almost insane irritation against them. . . . It looked sometimes as if wholesale massacres were prevented only by the presence of the Federal garrisons which were dispersed all over the country."

Upon Schurz's return, the president discouraged him from writing a report. Schurz went ahead and filed a full account. If Johnson read the report, it did not move him.

With the Freedmen's Bureau about to lapse, Congress wrote a new, more detailed bill, which would have continued the Sherman Land titles for three years and authorized Howard to grant forty-acre tracts. Plantation owners lobbied Johnson to veto the bill and to nullify Special Field Order 15. They wanted their plantations back. They knew that

Sherman was in town, and at the president's suggestion, they went to see him. They found him at Ulysses S. Grant's headquarters, conferring with Grant and several other generals. Grant invited them in, and they asked Sherman what he really meant by his order. It was just a temporary land transfer, Sherman said. The next day Johnson wrote to him, asking for a statement. Sherman replied, "I knew of course we could not convey title to land and merely provided 'possessory' titles, to be good as long as War and our Military Power lasted." With that sentence, Sherman all but erased Special Field Order 15.

The new Freedmen's Bill reached Johnson a few days later. He surprised Congress, vetoing the bill, the first sent to him to sign. Vetoes were rare. His veto was a sprawling, nearly four thousand–word all-points attack. He denied that the freedmen needed help, that there should be a Freedmen's Bureau in every county and parish running schools and asylums, renting and selling "landed estates" to freedmen, and imposing a court system empowered to fine or imprison whites who deprived freedmen of "any civil rights or immunities."

"Congress . . . has never founded schools for any class of our own people, not even for the orphans of those who have fallen in the defense of the Union, but has left the care of education to the much more competent and efficient control of the states, of communities, of private associations, and of individuals," Johnson wrote. "It has never deemed itself authorized to expend the public money for the rent or purchase of homes for the thousands, not to say millions, of the white race who are honestly toiling from day to day for their subsistence." The Constitution did not allow for "the support of indigent persons . . . nor can any good reason be advanced why, as a permanent establishment, it should be founded for one class or color of our people more than another." The freedmen did not need this large federal program. We underestimate their ability to "protect and take care of themselves," he said. Their "condition is not so exposed as may at first be imagined." And if jobs were scarce and times were hard in the South, they could move.

Radical Republicans, who were dedicated to black equality and suffrage, likened Johnson to someone who "ties up the children so that they shall not bite the rabid dog, and turns loose the rabid dog so that he can protect the children."

Congress failed to override his veto. They did write a new bill, but the promised forty acres had disappeared. All the freedmen received was a temporary stay against eviction until they had harvested their crops and were paid for any "betterments" they had made to the land. Freedmen were offered a chance to buy twenty-acre plots at $1.50 an acre on land the government held in South Carolina, money few had. Johnson vetoed the new bill as well, but this time Congress overrode his veto.

Johnson was undeterred. He refused to enforce the laws Congress passed. He moved quickly to set the rules for readmitting the Confederate states. In one of his first acts, he granted amnesty and a pardon to all rebels, excepting large landholders and Confederate officials. They had to appeal directly to the president. Within a year he pardoned seven thousand of the South's wealthiest—men he had once damned as a corrupt aristocracy. He had the Freedmen's Bureau's most effective assistant commissioners removed. The president "musters out all my officers," said a frustrated Howard. "I begin to tremble with anxiety for the freedmen," he wrote his wife.

"Thus Johnson defeats Congress at every point," said the Boston *Commonwealth*. "While Congress is passing acts to reconstruct the South, the president is driving a carriage and six through them."

V. "Nobody Knows the Trouble I See"—1865 and 1866

Johnson had all but conquered the Freedmen's Bureau in his first year in office. He got the better of Howard at every turn. He was a better tactician than the general. Howard had ordered his assistant commissioners to "select and set apart such confiscated and abandoned lands" for the freedmen "with as little delay as possible." "The pardon of the president will not be understood to extend to" this land, he instructed his staff on July 13, 1865. The next day he left the capital for a month's vacation in Maine. (He had not seen his family since early in the war.) The bureau was in the hands of his adjutant general, who undermined his order and was reporting directly to the president. Most of the assistant commissioners ignored the order. Had they acted, twenty thousand families could have received land.

In September, Johnson rescinded Howard's orders and any other instructions he had issued that interfered with the president's plans. The new order required that all land be returned to the owners he had pardoned. The White House wrote the order; it was signed and issued by Howard. The planters stormed the bureau, demanding their land. "Otis is the hardest worked man I ever saw," said his brother Rowland. "His office is full all of the time. . . . He is very busy now giving up their houses & land to them—the rebels."

Assistant Commissioner Rufus Saxton refused. He directed the bureau in South Carolina. He had been looking after the freedmen since he had settled forty thousand of them under Special Field Order 15. "Could a just government drive out these loyal men?" he protested. The land had been "solemnly pledged to the freedmen" by the bureau and the law. "Their love of the soil and desire to own farms amounts to a passion—it appears to be the dearest hope of their lives. I sincerely trust the government will never break its faith with a single one of these colonists by driving him from the home which he has been promised. It is of vital importance that our promises made to freedmen should be faithfully kept." He wasn't going to uproot them. "I cannot break faith with them," he said.

The president ordered Howard south to the land set aside by Sherman's order. He told him to arrange for "an agreement mutually satisfactory" between the former landholders and the freedmen. He meant for Howard to evict the freedmen and have them sign contracts to labor for their old enslavers. Johnson dictated his route. "Why did I not resign?" Howard asked in his autobiography. "Because I even yet strongly hoped in some way to befriend the freed people." His brother

Rowland knew how this trip saddened and burdened him. "He dreads it like death. How can he do it!" But Howard was a good soldier; he had good intentions. He followed his orders.

～

The freedmen gave Howard a hero's welcome. They crowded churches and homes, singing hymns like "On Jordan's Stormy Banks":

I am bound for the Promised Land
I am bound for the Promised Land;
Oh who will come and go with me?

They praised the bureau. They believed in General Howard as they had believed in Lincoln. They shared with him their dreams for the future. "You couldn't help tears, I know, when you should hear them speak freely of their wrongs & their hopes for themselves & their children," said Rowland.

Howard's arrival was a good omen. The freedmen believed that they would shortly have a home of their own—it was "a fixed and earnest conviction as strong as any belief a man can ever have," said an officer of the Freedman's Bureau. Sherman's field order had set the precedent; on Sherman's march, soldiers had told them they were free to take over the plantations. Rumors were sweeping the South that the new year would begin with the Freedmen's Bureau opening a "great document" closed with "four seals" to reveal the government's "final orders" to divide the plantations. As one Virginia freedman reasoned, "if you had the right to take the master's [slaves], you had the right to take master's land, too." Some had taken over the "masters'" mansions as the Union forces advanced. On one Mississippi plantation, freedmen divided the land and the tools among themselves. Some refused to sign contracts for work; they were waiting for land. A few had banked money with someone they trusted, saving for the big day. In one North Carolina town one hundred fifty couples had married to ensure they would be eligible for land. Only land will allow "the poor class to enjoy the sweet boon of freedom," said newly emancipated Merrimon Howard. It was land that Harriet Tubman used to encourage those fleeing slavery to board the Union gunboats during an 1863 raid on plantations. She sang:

Come along! Come along! Don't be alarmed,
Uncle Sam is rich enough to give you all a farm.

To which the now free men and women shouted, *Glory.*

At Charleston's Colored School, seven hundred children were gathered to sing to their honored visitors, the general and his brother:

I have a father in the Promised Land . . .
I'll away, I'll away to the Promised Land

But Howard was there on an errand from the landlord. He stopped in Charleston and then left for Edisto Island on a sidewheel steamer, the *Planter*, owned by the bureau. Robert Smalls had escaped from slavery by seizing this ship in one of the most celebrated acts of heroism in the war. He went on to pilot the ship for the navy, and he was piloting it now. He would later serve in Congress. This was a return trip for Howard. Freedmen and their families had been farming on the Sea Islands since 1862, when the plantation owners evacuated before the Union arrived, leaving them behind. He had enjoyed his earlier visit to inspect the Port Royal Experiment. "Those interesting people are comparatively happy; they work diligently, they raise good crops and they are more prosperous than they ever dared to hope for in their wildest dreams," he said. About one thousand families, fifty-three hundred people in all, were farming on Edisto and the small islands nearby.

When his boat landed, eighteen freedmen dashed to meet him, riding assorted horses and mules. They lined up in two rows for a proper military reception. Howard was traveling with two former slave owners from the island. Their presence was unexpected and alarming. The rebels had returned to take over again, said the first man to see the boat. "The word passed like lightning along the line and such a change as came over them," reported Elizabeth Botume, a teacher for the New England Freedmen's Aid Society. "They were loud in their denunciations, and declared they would not submit to it."

Howard and his traveling party were seated in an ambulance wagon pulled by "four fine white horses." The men saluted as they went by and then joined the procession. At the churchyard, the men again formed two lines and saluted the general. Inside the Episcopal Church, two thousand freedmen and the island's teachers were waiting.

He told them why he was there straight away. He was there to take their land. President Johnson said they had to give it back. He asked them to agree to work for their old masters. He said that the bureau would insure that they were treated fairly. The whipping post was a thing of the past. He looked out upon "dissatisfaction and sorrow" in "every part of the assembly," he recalled. "My address . . . met with no apparent favor."

The room erupted. "No! No!" they cried out. "We can't do it!" "Never! No, Never!" They refused to work again for "the Secesh." They spoke to him with "rough eloquence," said Howard, recalling the scene forty years later. Their words had stayed with him: "One very black man, thick set, and strong, cried out from the gallery: 'Why, General Howard, why do you take away our lands? You take them from us who are true, always true to the government! You give them to our all-time enemies! That is not right!'" Another said, I have lived all my life with a basket over my head. Now that basket is gone and there is sunlight. He would not have that basket lowered over him again.

"They looked so sad and, shook their heads so mournfully, many of them leaving the church. General Howard was much affected, and begged them to stay and hear him out," said Botume.

He asked them to forgive the slave owners. Their old masters had been pardoned; they were coming back. Set aside your bitterness and forgive them. He put it to a vote, asking for a show of hands. Who was willing to forgive? Who was unwilling? A few hands were raised each time. "He said the ayes had it, but I could not see much difference,"

Botume said. He said that as the head of the bureau, he had their best interests at heart. How many were willing to trust him? "All hands went up." Consider the owners, he pleaded. They deserved to be reunited with their homes. The owners on the mainland had been pardoned and returned to their land. Why should Edisto Island be any different? General Sherman had only placed them here by "military necessity" to get them out of the way, he said. The war was over; everything had changed. "It all seemed like sophistry, and as if he was trying to persuade himself as well as them," Botume said.

They didn't have "absolute title," he insisted. They were just "occupying the homesteads." He "urged them to make the best terms they could" with the plantation owners. He asked them to pick three people to represent them and come to an agreement. A committee left the assembly with Howard's brother to read them the official papers (though they had secretly learned to read when they were enslaved).

The meeting broke down into "noise and confusion," said Howard. The school superintendent asked them to sing. They answered with "Wandering in the Wilderness of Sorrow and Gloom." They didn't want to sing anymore. "I'se so torn in my mind, I can't sing," said one. But one old woman, off to the side, started singing, in a "sweet voice," "Nobody Knows the Trouble I See." Everyone joined in, swaying in unison, keeping time by nodding their heads and moving their feet, as they sang.

> *Nobody knows de trouble I see*
> *Nobody knows but Jesus*

They were putting their faith in God; they were putting their faith in the Christian general. He wept.

> *Sometimes I'm up, sometimes I'm down*
> *Sometimes I'm almost on de groun'*

The song was a favorite at the end of the Civil War in Charleston's Black schools, where it was sung as "Nobody Knows the Trouble I've

Had." It was picked up on the Sea Islands, of which Edisto was one, and changed a little, just as it would change again as it was sung into the next centuries.

> *What makes ole Satan hate me so?*
> *Because he got me once and he let me go*

The committee returned. "On no condition" would they work again for slaveholders. They would not return to slavery in any form. They wanted to rent and, over time with the money raised from their crops of corn, cotton, and rice, to buy their farms.

Howard persisted. He had one of the former slave owners speak. "He had been a hard master, leaving his slaves to the . . . most merciless overseer," said Botume. "He took a look all around upon these blacks, whom he had probably never seen before under such circumstances— free to come and go, and in a church belonging to the whites—and there was quite a sensation visible both on his part and theirs as he looked at them," she said. He said that he saw the faces of his old slaves. He wished to hire them. He had the capital, they had the labor, he said. "He had been pardoned for all that he had done, if he had ever done anything wrong. He said this in a tone of pleasantry, with a grin on his face, as though it were a good joke!" said Botume.

One of the freedmen stood up to answer him. "If he was sincere and honest . . . he ought to set off a thousand acres and give it to the children of the poor black people who had suffered so under slavery."

Howard rose and replied, saying "he was sorry to hear him speak in such an unchristian spirit; that he himself professed to be a follower of Christ, who taught us to forgive our enemies; and said that he had been in twenty-two battles, had lost his arm, and been severely wounded many times; he was willing to suffer more, if necessary, and yet he forgave them, from the bottom of his heart," reported Botume. "I thought it would be a little easier for him to forgive them for what he had voluntarily exposed himself to, than for them who were crushed every day of their lives."

A chaplain offered a prayer and the meeting adjourned.

∼

"Why, General Howard, why do you take away our lands?" The freedmen walked away from the meeting searching for answers. They asked their teachers to explain. They studied the Bible. Their teachers read to them from Exodus. The Israelites were freed from slavery into forty years of troubles. They knew this story. *As the Israelites were departing boldly, the Egyptians gave chase to them, and all the chariot horses of Pharaoh, his horsemen and warriors over took them encamped by the sea.* Exodus was a contemporary story.

Howard returned to Charleston by nightfall, moved by what he had heard. He wired Stanton telling him that "they will submit, but with evident sorrow, to the breaking of the promise of General Sherman's order. . . . My task is a hard one, and I am convinced that something must be done to give these people and others the prospect of home-steads."

Stanton wrote back, telling him to stall, a basic strategy of bureau-crats but something that didn't seem to occur to Howard. "I do not un-derstand that your orders require you to disturb the freedmen in the possession at present, but only ascertain whether a just, mutual agree-ment can be made between the pardoned owners and the Freedmen, and if it can, then carry it into effect," Stanton wrote. If they couldn't agree, leave them be. Stanton was opposed to moving any freedmen off the "Sherman Reservation."

Howard thought it over, seeking a compromise, as usual. The par-doned landowners would have to a sign an "obligation" to draw up fair contracts and not interfere with the freedmen's schools, he decided. He hoped they would act with a "spirit of liberality and humanity." He gave the freedmen a deadline: sign contracts in two months or leave. The freedmen would be protected by a "Board of Supervisors" com-posed of a representative from the bureau, the planters, and the freed-men. But the owners refused because they would never confer with a "colored man" as their equal. They would rather have their land "sink to perdition." Howard had specified that "citizens" serve on the board; Blacks, they said, were not "citizens." They protested and had the army investigate.

The committee of freedmen created at the meeting had also thought things over. They wrote to Howard:

"General, it is with painful hearts that we the committee address you," they began. They could not sign the order turning over their land.

"General we want homesteads; we were promised homesteads by the government. If it does not carry out the promises its agents made to us, if the government having concluded to befriend its late enemies and to neglect to observe the principles of common faith between its self and us its allies in the war you said was over . . . we are left in a more unpleasant condition than our former.

"We are at the mercy of those who are combined to prevent us from getting land enough to lay our Fathers bones upon. We have property in horses, cattle, carriages, and articles of furniture, but we are landless and homeless. . . . You will see this is not the condition of really freemen.

"You ask us to forgive the land owners of our island. *You* only lost your right arm in war and might forgive them. The man who tied me to a tree and gave me thirty-nine lashes and who stripped and flogged my mother and my sister and who will not let me stay in his empty hut except I will do his planting and be satisfied with his price and who combines with others to keep away land from me well knowing I would not have anything to do with him if I had land of my own—that man, I cannot well forgive. Does it look as if he has forgiven me, seeing how he tries to keep me in a condition of helplessness?

"General . . . help us to reach land where we shall not be slaves nor compelled to work for those who would treat us as such. . . . Landless, homeless, voteless, we can only pray to god and hope for *his help, your influence and assistance.*"

Howard answered, holding out hope even as he lectured them once more. "You are right *in wanting homesteads* and will *surely be defended in the possession of every one* which you shall purchase or have already purchased. The government does not wish to befriend its enemies and injure its friends," but the plantation owners have been forgiven, and returned to full citizenship. "The duty of forgiveness is plain and simple. Forgive as we hope to be forgiven of Him who governs all things," he wrote. For the present, it was best they sign contracts. The Board of Supervisors will "not permit what you fear. The old masters would be very foolish to try a system of oppression as it would ruin them forever now that you are free." Some these of contracts can be leases. "I do not think the planters will object to leasing you land," he said, oblivious of the planters' attitude. In the meantime, he promised to take their case to Congress and the president. "Congress must meet before any public lands can be had and before I can buy any for you. I will ask for your rights and try to obtain them. . . . Send your petition to Congress, if you wish, and I will see that it is not passed by without proper attention. The president himself will urge something in your behalf."

"With deep sorrow," the committee of freedmen petitioned President Johnson:

"Here is where secession was born and nurtured. Here is where we have toiled nearly all our lives as slaves and were treated like dumb driven cattle. This is our home. We have made these lands what they are. We were the only true and loyal people that were found in possession of these lands. We have been always ready to strike for liberty and humanity, yea to fight if needs be to preserve this glorious union. Shall not we who are freedman and have been always true to this Union have the same rights as are enjoyed by others? Have we broken any law of these United States? Have we forfeited our rights of property in land? . . .

"We the freedmen of this island and of the State of South Carolina do therefore petition to you as the President of these United States, that some provisions be made by which every colored man can purchase land and hold it as his own. We wish to have a home if it be but a few acres. . . .

"We pray that god will direct your heart in making such provision for us as freedmen which will tend to unite these states together stronger than ever before. May God bless you in the administration of your duties as the President of these United States is the humble prayer of us all."

Howard was true to his word; he tried to save their land on Edisto. He met with Johnson to argue their case. The President was not persuaded. A couple of months earlier he had proposed a compromise to Johnson: the plantations could be returned if the owners set aside a homestead of five to ten acres for each family. Johnson was "amused," Howard said. Howard also wrote two provisions for the bill that would reauthorize the bureau. One would grant the freedmen on the Sea Islands and the coast their farms as long as the head of each family was alive. The second provision would have let the government buy the Sea Island plantations to rent or sell them to the freedmen.

The first provision was stripped from the bill before it reached the floor. Howard, caving in to the planters' demands after they all met with the president, had returned some of the plantations. He also removed the Black representative from the supervising board. The other provision, to buy land for the freedmen, was part of the bill that passed. Johnson vetoed the bill, and the idea sank from sight. He visited Johnson once more to plead for the Edisto freedmen, but the former slave owners had won.

Howard had started out intending to bring freedom and equality to a land blighted by slavery. Sherman was right: it was a task for Hercules, not any mortal. Now he worked daily to break the promise of giving freedmen their forty acres. He was always looking for a compromise. He wanted to accommodate the President, the southern planters, the freedmen. He thought reason would prevail. But it was Howard who was compromised. In the end, after all his promises, he gave Edisto back to the planters. Four months after his visit, soldiers and agents from the bureau landed on the island to evict the freedmen. They fought back with shovels and pick axes; the army retreated. The soldiers returned another day and removed the freedmen. Many had already given up and left for the mainland.

Throughout Sherman Land, and anywhere Blacks had settled on confiscated land, they were evicted. The army removed most of the twenty thousand freedmen in southeast Virginia. In Louisiana, Black farmers were ordered off sixty-two thousand acres. In South Carolina's low country, they put up a fight. "They would die where they stood before they would surrender their claims to the land," they told a newspaper. Their leader was arrested; those unwilling to sign labor contracts were evicted. In all, only about two thousand freedmen in Georgia and South Carolina held on to the land they had been promised.

By spring 1866, Johnson had returned 414,652 acres to the planters, including land that had been given to freedmen. He fired Saxton. He was dismissed with a terse note from Howard. Freedmen, upon hearing that their ally Saxton had been removed, held large rallies in his honor, rallies he couldn't bear to attend. They sang his praises, softening his name to Saxaby, and putting him in a popular hymn:

> *General Saxaby a sittin' on de tree of life,*
> *Roll, Jordan, roll*

He was in heaven. They were crossing the Jordan to freedom.

Thousands of South Carolina freedmen gave pennies and nickels in tribute to their great friend. As Saxton walked alone down the wharf feeling "defeated and disgraced" to board a steamer north, a group of freedmen came forward to present their warrior with a sword.

We have "no land, no house, not so much as place to lay our head," the former Mississippi slave Merrimon Howard wrote to the man who shared his last name. We are "brothers on the battlefield, but in the peaceful pursuits of life it seems that we are strangers."

In the great Washington victory parade at the war's end, Howard rode alongside Sherman at the head of the army of the West. People cheered for him, calling out his name. He then sat with Sherman, Grant, and President Johnson in the reviewing stand. His lectures would pack churches, but after a couple of years heading the Freedmen's Bureau, his reputation dwindled. He could not fill a church anymore, he said. He stayed with the Freedmen's Bureau even as it was hobbled, suffering from a lack of field staff and clear direction from him. His staff was often confused about what he wanted them to do. He lacked basic political sense. But he believed that he had made the right concessions. "After years of thinking and observation I'm inclined to believe that the restoration of their lands to the planters proved for all their future better for the negroes."

His renown had faded and he had accumulated political enemies—the bureau had been viewed with suspicion from the day it first passed the House by only two votes. In the bureau's waning years, his enemies pursued Howard with two investigations and three civil suits. In the House he faced fifteen charges, including improperly using government funds for Howard University, for which he was a leading founder and later the university president. He was exonerated of all charges only to face a lengthy Military Court of Inquiry a few years later. This time he had to answer for the accounting irregularities of his disbursing officer. He was again acquitted, but was under fire once more in civil suits wanting him to repay $189,000 to the War Department.

The cases were dismissed, but after years of stories about the scandalous "Freedmen's Ring," the public associated Howard's bureau with fraud and deceit. This belief was hardened by a generation of historians who portrayed the bureau as a colossal waste. Howard and his family fled Washington. He went west to fight Indians. He chased Chief Joseph and hundreds of families for four months through the Northern Rockies in the Nez Perce War, until Chief Joseph surrendered, saying "I will fight no more forever." In the East he had helped a persecuted people; in the West he was a persecutor. If he saw a contradiction, he didn't say. He had only gone to war after his negotiations failed.

Howard was "an honest man with too much faith in human nature," said W. E. B. Dubois. "He was sympathetic and humane, and tried with endless application and desperate sacrifice to do a hard, thankless duty." For Dubois, "the Freedmen's Bureau was the most extraordinary and far-reaching institution of social uplift that America has ever attempted," he wrote in 1935. If the war had gone on for another year, the freedmen's communities may have had time to take hold, says one historian. But the war ended within a few weeks, Lincoln was assassinated, and Johnson shut down the bureau's land redistribution. "To have given each one of the million Negro free families a forty-acre freehold would have made a basis of real democracy in the United States that might easily have transformed the modern world," said Dubois.

Within months of Sherman's granting forty acres, his promise was revoked. The bureau never had as much land as its critics said. Howard did the math: "About one–five hundredth (.002) only of the entire amount of land in the insurrectionary districts has ever been held, and had the plan of assigning it to freedmen been carried out, the bureau would have been unable to furnish an acre per family." The bureau had, briefly, 850,000 acres. At the same time, the government gave the railroads more than 67 million acres.

Less than 5 percent of the Black population acquired land in the first years after the war. It was too little. But even that was too much.

VI. What is Freedom?—Then, Now, and Forever

What is slavery and what is freedom? Sherman and Stanton had asked the twenty men, freeborn and formerly enslaved, who had gathered for the Savannah Colloquy. Slavery is taking the work of another man; freedom is reaping the fruit of your own labor, they answered. And with that answer they defined the challenge of the years after the Civil War.

Freedom was more than the absence of chains, yes, but just what was required to make people truly free? Americans were confused, and stumbled over a word they claimed almost as their own invention.

Land was essential and withheld. "The tragedy of Reconstruction is the failure of the black masses to acquire land," said historian Claude F. Oubre. Without land, "the freedmen were soon deprived of the political and civil rights which they had won."

Against great odds, Blacks acquired land and, in places, a taste of prosperity. By 1900, 25 percent of Black farmers owned their land. That ownership peaked in 1910, but then the tide went out fast. Farms everywhere were disappearing. Black farms were lost at such a fast rate that "it was almost as if the earth was opening up and swallowing black farmers," said historian Pete Daniel. An estimated 85 percent of Black-owned farmland in the South has disappeared since 1969. Perhaps half of that has been lost due to "partition sales," in which land that was jointly inherited by a family, but without a legal will, is sold out from under them to the highest bidder. Today, the five largest white landowners in America together own more rural land than all of Black America combined.

What is freedom? One answer is forty acres, a mule, and the chance to benefit from your own labor. It's citizenship—the vote, equal justice. Or maybe it's a quarter acre, a split-level house, a decent job, two kids in a good school, a three-year-old Ford in the driveway. The Promised Land doesn't have to be grand, doesn't have to be a shining city upon the hill, but it has to be fair. The pursuit of happiness is America's Promised Land.

Moses stood outside the Promised Land just once, but the emancipated slaves, the freedmen, were denied again and again.

SEEKING PEACE

Peace by the Quarter Acre

Veterans Memorial Highway, Veterans Memorial Coliseum, Veterans Memorial Playing Field. The veterans named the Long Island landscape. World War II was assumed; it was *the* war. The memorials didn't talk about Civil War veterans or Korean War veterans. This was their island to make after the war.

World War II was only ten years distant when my parents moved into their new house and only seventeen years past when I started school. The war towered over us. We played war in our backyards and in the woods, mimicking the sounds of shooting and explosions that we had seen on the TV show *Combat!* We had plastic rifles and bazookas and grenades and plastic helmets with plastic camouflage leaves. At age six we asked each other if we were going to join the army, Air Force, or navy, the way kids in private schools must sort between Harvard and Yale. Fighting in a world war just seemed like something grownups did. For one birthday party I took seven friends to watch the new movie about D-Day.

"They'll never stop fighting that war," my father said.

～

Two suitcases in the basement were the only clues about my parents' lives before they moved into their new house. With the exception of some furniture from their apartment, this was all they had taken from their city lives.

By the time I came upon the suitcases, they were dusty, sunken relics—one lying with its side caved in. In my father's suitcase was his high-school class picture in a sepia tone (Monroe High; school paper: the *Monroe Doctrine*), his framed diploma, some books of engineering tables and drawings from an early postwar job refitting part of the Panama Canal. His Air Force uniform was hanging, uncovered, under the stairs.

My mother's suitcase had some schoolbook exercises in her perfect penmanship and a scrapbook of pictures of movie stars that she had clipped out of magazines. I'd heard of some of them, but many others are remembered now only in scrapbooks like these. She had made this scrapbook in her early teens. It was the dream book of a child in the Great Depression.

A slim gathering from their former lives. I asked my father once about the suitcases: Why weren't there more? He said, "When we moved out here, that's when our lives began."

Founding Story

The house I grew up in had the bare basics of suburban-hood: one picture window, three bedrooms, one bathroom, kitchen, dining room opening to the living room, unfinished basement, narrow garage for one car, small backyard and slim side yards—there was only twelve feet between houses. The house was about 850 square feet, half the size of the average house built twenty years later, houses with more space in the "entrance foyer" than our dining room.

In 1954, my father and mother followed the Northern State Parkway until it ran out. They got off at the next-to-last exit that had opened, about forty miles from the city. They bought a new house in a development on flat potato fields, a large tract of twisting streets grandly named Valmont. There was nothing much around but farms. My father drove his father out from the Bronx to see the house. Long before they arrived, his father said, "I always wanted you to have a house in the country—but in *this* country."

The house cost $14,000. No shrubs, no trees, no lawns at that point. Telephone poles, wires, and each house with a TV antenna clamped to the chimney. They were like houses set down in a sandbox. Between the houses you could see a long way across the flatness.

A friend at work told him to look at houses there. My parents liked what they saw and put down a deposit. One day after work, he went to check on the construction. He was in the bathroom when he thought: "I didn't order black and green tile. I'm going to find that builder." He was in the house next door.

After my parents bought the house, they had just $38 left in their joint account. But it wasn't a "stretch" he said. They could cover the mortgage.

Their neighbors were Irish and Italian, children of immigrants in the first house any of them had ever owned. Telephone line workers, custodians, factory workers. My dad was an engineer. There were many other engineers, a few cops, teachers, and one doctor, an anomaly, who, it was said, had helped many people. There were many Catholics, Protestants, of course, a smattering of Jews. All white, all married. Years later there were a couple of widows and a rumor of a divorce far off, many streets away.

They were mostly blue collar, working class, but they did not think of themselves that way, I'm sure. They had a house, a yard, a car, a mortgage. They were middle class.

They planted lawns, bought lawn mowers, had very few tools. Each Father's Day led to the Sears hardware department. My father and the other fathers "tuned up" their own cars, working in the driveway, gapped the spark plugs, used a "timing light," an arcane procedure that often ended up with several men leaning in under the hood, an automotive priesthood.

They were working to achieve the paradise promised by the home handyman magazines. My father had a stack of them in his nightstand by the bed for years. The same year or two's worth, ca. 1954–1955, the year they moved in. The magazines sat there for decades. This was the peg board, knotty pine, paneling, family-room era. Room for the growing family! Entertain friends! Build an all-in-one entertainment center! It was a big era for all-in-one projects, whether for the homeowner or the city planner: Clear slums! Build new highways! End poverty forever! All-in-one solutions were the rage.

Some men had already "finished" their basements, making workshops, playrooms, and bars, all in close proximity. Basements were the frontiers, the promise of new things, a little domestic chunk of Manifest Destiny.

~

My parents moved in just before Thanksgiving. All the relatives came for Thanksgiving, even though they didn't yet have a refrigerator. They kept all the food on the back steps and a cat came along and dined on the turkey, a story that has become a Thanksgiving tradition.

The houses in the neighborhood were sparsely furnished: one black-and-white television; one phone, black with a dial. Later on you could add a "princess" phone (with a choice of colors!) on an "extension line." One car—Ford, GM, or Chrysler—even if there were two drivers. One family had a Rambler and another a Studebaker, slightly odd, like buying week-old bread. A couple of families had two cars. Only a few moms worked. It was a binary world: work or home, Coke or Pepsi, Democrat or Republican, Free World or Communism, Christ or not, white or not.

~

Small houses, but each big enough, and bigger really than their square-foot measure. The defining measure is in those few feet between the houses. Each house stood alone, a miniature ranch or estate. If you had offered prospective buyers a bigger house, but one that was joined to its neighbors, most people would opt for a smaller, independent house.

House hunting, they had all weighed the options—hardwood floors and floor plans and schools that were mostly unbuilt—but it's those few feet of separation that they were buying. Small distances meant a great deal.

In best-selling books, sociologists were quick to damn the barracks-like rows of suburban houses with their wrist-thin spindly maples, but they missed the promise of having your own place and your own yard. We lived under a cloud of approbation. We had been judged banal, ticky-tacky, conformist. All that striving and dreaming, mortgages, and car payments were, in the eyes of the critics and sociologists, just blight.

They all started out together. They were all learning about being homeowners. You couldn't call "the super" to fix something. You called Dick next door or Lester across the street or Murray around the corner for help. Some of them were real "handymen"—the highest accolade. They could fix anything.

If there were a domestic emergency, Frances or Virginia would step in, help with the kids or dinner. It was routine then; it seems remarkable now, this fine art of keeping out of other people's business but being there in good times and bad. They were good neighbors. It's like the front lawns: each distinct, yet joining together.

There were kids everywhere. Kids playing tag or hide and seek or stick ball, or riding bikes, playing until dark. On summer nights the neighbors would be out, gardening, tinkering, visiting; my dad and Lester sitting at the head of the driveway in lawn chairs drinking a couple of beers, the moths thick under the streetlight. Hot nights, all windows open.

There were big parades on Memorial Day and for the start of the Little League season, Little Leaguers marching for blocks and blocks in wavy rows, Boy Scouts and Girl Scouts, Webelos and Cub Scouts,

Brownies, marching bands, baton twirlers, fire engines, and police cars. Kids marching to please adults. The men didn't march; they'd had enough of that.

Forty Miles—The Commute to "The City"

The Long Island Railroad, morning and evening.

A.M.: The hour of aftershave and mouthwash, toothpaste and deodorant, perfume and scented soaps. The smell of coffee and the sweet inkyness of the morning newspapers. Crisp, dry-cleaned shirts. Polished shoes. Ties knotted.

P.M.: Hour of ambiguity. The army returns, exhausted. The smell of sweat, beer, Manhattan grit, stale coffee, and cigarette breath.

The Bar Car: Dashing Dan—once the railroad's commuter hero—became Desperate Dan. The Bar Car was jam-packed and thick with smoke. Rapid-fire drinking, like a football team rushing the ball up the field in the closing minutes. Here the "two-minute drill" was a rush to drink, to smoke, and to drink some more. I had seen the bar car a few times on trips to the city: I didn't want to grow up to be any of those guys.

New Houses (1200 Square Feet)

There were still many farms around. Every farm became a "development." The new houses were a little larger, had an extra room or two, another garage. But it was all the same, like going from a Ford to a Plymouth. Only the details differed.

There were new model homes out on the Vets Highway. They were mobbed every Sunday. People visited these houses just as people in other parts of the country take a Sunday drive to the mountains. They enjoyed the view; they liked to think about the possibilities, liked to consider "moving up." Back home a few might even sit down and "crunch the numbers" to see if they could carry a bigger mortgage. (Or "make a bigger nut" as the commuters on the train said.)

People also turned out to see the new cars when they arrived each fall at the dealers' showrooms. When someone came home with a new car, the neighbors came over to admire it, everyone gathering around on the driveway, as if they expected the car to speak. The owner would open the doors so everyone could take in that new car smell. He'd raise the hood and maybe take his neighbors for a ride down to the Carvel. (*No ice cream in the car!*)

"See the USA in Your Chevrolet"

Vacations were car trips. Many people went to visit relatives upstate or in the Midwest. No one got on an airplane to go anywhere. In junior high school I had one friend whose family flew to England one summer. That was a big trip and we marveled at their tales of the exotic Brits. They carried around their photo album for months.

I had only one friend whose family had forged the Mississippi and driven coast to coast. Driving that far with a back seat stuffed with squirming kids took some fortitude. (*Are we there yet?*) With open windows—few cars had air conditioning—you baked in the August heat and the road dirt. For diversion there was only the push-button AM car radio to pull in the local stations. The interstate highways were still under construction. Old roads, like parts of Route 66, were in their last, shabby days. Breakdowns were common enough, as was getting lost, losing maps, and looking for gas stations at night in shuttered towns with the needle on empty. My friend's car had overheated in Death Valley, and Kansas had almost swallowed them alive. When I asked them about crossing those flat states, they said that I just wouldn't understand.

But mostly people stuck close to home through the long summer. Vacations for working dads were usually only two weeks, and no one we knew went away on the weekends. On the long evenings the whole family might go to play miniature golf or to the driving range, or in the heat surrender the family meal—meat and overcooked, limp green beans—to a kid's appetite: burgers and fries, pizza, Chinese food, or hot dogs steamed in beer, which was one summer's fad.

Summer meant hanging around with friends, going to the beach, going to the movies. (Some theaters still hung out banners boasting, in snow-capped letters, "Air Conditioned!") No one I knew went to summer camp, or had any kind of lessons beyond swimming lessons. We were left to ourselves.

The Nightly News

Everyone watched the nightly news: Cronkite or Huntley and Brinkley. There were about seven TV stations: three networks, two local, "Educational TV," and UHF, which no one ever saw. No need for a remote. You walked over to the TV, which was usually housed in a big "Colonial" hutch just like the Founding Fathers had, and twisted a dial. Those hutches and cabinets housed a glowing city of tubes. The television would have to "warm up," we said, and when you turned it off, the picture shrank to a dot as if it were rocketing off to the far recesses of the solar system.

When the president addressed the nation, all three networks carried it and usually returned to "regular programming" after a brief, strenuously objective summary. When a show was popular it wallpapered the culture; everyone talked about it. Johnny Carson was on late, 11:30, but his jokes were common currency the next day.

Most everyone read a newspaper: *Newsday* for purported liberals, the more conservative *Long Island Press*, or the *Suffolk Sun* in the morning with off-register color comics. In the city they read different newspapers. Most everyone subscribed to the same magazines: *Life* or *Look*, *Time* or *Newsweek* (or even *US News & World Report*, the Studebaker of the newsweeklies), *TV Guide*, *Reader's Digest*, *National Geographic*, *Popular Science*, or the lowly *Popular Mechanics*, and the ladies' magazines like the *Ladies' Home Journal* with "Can This Marriage Be Saved?" which I read closely. It was a rare patch of private life breaking out in public. You saw it only in a few places like Dear Abby or Ask Ann Landers. The culture was male, made up of official statements by experts. The personal wasn't yet political; it was still personal.

Free World or Godless Communism

In my earliest school memories, our teacher is telling us that "we might be attacked today" or she is saying that we were practicing an attack, a distinction lost on a six-year-old. This may have been part of the "air raid drills" we had in the jumpy aftermath of the Cuban Missile Crisis. We'd be lined up in the halls facing the wall. It felt like each and every one of us was being punished for doing something wrong.

And then President Kennedy was shot and somebody shot somebody else. School was closed. We played all day. Not an adult anywhere moved. They were slumped in front of the TV. I'd go in and out of my friends' houses and it was the same scene: their parents sitting silently, sitting motionless as if they had come to rest at the bottom of the sea.

Assassinations became a regular thing. We'd be out on the playground for recess and somebody would come out and lower the flag to half-staff again. What happened? we asked. It's MLK, it's RFK, we were told. Not much was explained to us. Our teachers didn't understand it either.

~

The Cold War permeated everything, like the smell of gasoline on clothes.

Cuba was a dagger pointed at America. Soviet leaders were crude men who rapped a shoe on the desk at the UN, shouting, "We will bury you." They still wore hats and drove out-of-date funereal black cars. They had parades to review rows and rows of missiles and tanks rolling by. We had parades with floats made of roses and inflatable cartoon characters sailing down Manhattan's streets to Macy's. They wanted to dominate the world. We only wanted people to be happy, to vote, to have a house and a car and a Coke.

In the movies we saw, the Russians were vodka-drinking oafs. They'd swagger and bluster, only to stir up their vodka-loaded selves too much and fall down. We were lean Gary Coopers and Gregory

Pecks. Pragmatic, at ease, with a sense of humor. All these movies were Westerns in different costumes. The Russians were the black hats come to town. This is how it looked to a child in Cuba Hill Elementary School. (It was built on a hill named for Teddy Roosevelt's charge up San Juan Hill with the Rough Riders.)

Cuba Hill was a one-story, red-brick, flat-roofed school. Inside, the cinderblock walls were painted dark red and that chalky "eye ease" green that you still see at motor vehicle bureaus and old hospitals.

We sang "My Country 'Tis of Thee" every morning in the first and second grade. *My country 'tis of thee, sweet land of liberty. . . .* We sang the Cold War ballad "Freedom Isn't Free"—*You've got to pay a price, you've got to sacrifice*—at our grade school moving-up exercises, along with "The Impossible Dream." I think our class picked that one; it was on Broadway then.

And this was where a teacher in the fourth grade, pointing at a map of the USSR, said, "You can see how they would want to expand." After class, I asked her: Couldn't you point at a map of the USA and say the same thing? The next day, she corrected herself in front of the class.

FBI at the Door

One summer day, two FBI agents came to the door. They wanted to ask my mother a few questions.

My father was an engineer, along with about half of Long Island, and he did defense work (ditto). On the Cold War checklists, his father came up as someone suspicious to be watched. He had been born in Russia (maybe) and was a member of a communist union. Actually, he was born in Lithuania or Poland or Russia—that flat corner that kept changing hands. He walked across Europe to escape the Cossacks and the draft and came to America before World War I. When he worked as a tailor he had joined the union of necessity, which was the Workmen's Circle, socialists said to be left of left. (*Der Abiter Ring* observed May Day and the anniversary of the Russian Revolution as holidays, but not Yom Kippur.) He himself was a man of the prayer book and the pinochle deck. I never heard him talk politics. He didn't let my father join the Boy Scouts because he hated uniforms—he didn't come to this country to dress up children like soldiers—but that's his only political statement that I know of. He also once scolded my father for missing a vote. "You don't know what you've got here," he had said. "Where I came from you couldn't vote. It's a sin not to vote."

What did my mother tell the FBI agents? Did she say that, yes, he had been a tailor and he had sewn her some beautiful hats? Or did she say, yes, you're on to us: immigrants are born in other countries.

The FBI agents impressed us kids. Short haircuts, suits, thin ties. Just like the TV show. We regarded them as if they had the powers of superheroes. They probably knew everything already, but there was nothing much to know around our neighborhood. It was just cool to see them.

Christ or Not

When my parents moved in, they put a mezuzah up on the doorframe at the front and back doors. A mezuzah houses a small scroll with the central prayer of morning and evening services, the Shema Yisrael: "Hear, O Israel: the Lord is our God, the Lord is one." The mezuzah was small, no more than three inches tall. You could go in and out of the house for years and never notice it, and yet some of my parents' Jewish friends told them not to put it up.

This was still an era of widespread, accepted antisemitism. In the army Airforce, my father was in Florida for training, being marched past hotels with signs that said: No Jews Allowed. He and his friends had at one point or another been called "Christ killers" and other names. By the 1950s the name-calling was fading, but antisemitism lived on, cloaked in quotas. Elite schools limited the Jews they admitted; many jobs, it was supposed to be understood, were for Christians only. And it was understood that Jews didn't live in some neighborhoods and towns. "Are there any members of our tribe there?" a Jew would ask another. The ghetto walls had fallen, but there are many ways to build new walls. I'm sure that was on my parents' minds when they were looking for a house.

In Hebrew school our teachers were still reeling from the Holocaust, which was then not even twenty years past. They hadn't found the words to talk about it, to teach it. Without any introduction or background they made us watch the unedited, black-and-white documentary footage from Auschwitz and Buchenwald: emaciated prisoners staring right into the camera, piles of naked, skeletal bodies, piles of shoes and hair and teeth. Some teachers would say nothing after this, some would yell at us. For what? For "assimilating," for not being Jewish enough.

One teacher challenged us: Are you a Jewish American or an American Jew? The message was: Don't get too comfortable. Jews always have to leave. You're not home; you're in exile. We were eight, nine, ten years old, being sent to more school after school. We just wanted to go outside and play.

White or Not

We had a practice race riot in the third grade, a reenactment of the nightly news. In all of Cuba Hill, among maybe seven hundred kids in six grades and kindergarten, there was only one black kid, Kim. He was talented on stage, and sometimes starred in our plays. I knew him and we were friendly with his family. He's gone to Hollywood where he has appeared in many films and hundreds of TV shows. He also writes screenplays and commercials.

One day at recess, kids started linking arms with other kids. I looked up and a big chain of kids was chasing down Kim. I don't know how it started; I was one of maybe only three or four kids on the playground who was not involved. All of a sudden, parts of the playground emptied out, basketballs and kickballs were abandoned, and the chase was on. Kim took off running hard. The flying wedge of kids cornered him. He stood his ground and demanded to know who started this. When that kid stepped forward, Kim punched him in the eye. The teachers raced in to break it up.

For some reason, it fell to the gym teacher to lecture us. He didn't talk about race and respect, or about civil rights and equality. He tried to scare us straight with stories about Sing Sing, the famous prison where, even if we could get over the walls, we couldn't escape across the electrified railroad tracks. If we didn't straighten up, we were all going to Sing Sing. His lecture was a masterpiece of stupidity. We drew no lesson about how the whiteness of our suburb was founded on racist housing policy. That was invisible to us.

Moon Shot

My mind was elsewhere—on the moon and the stars. I was caught up in the "Space Race." Other boys knew baseball players and their statistics; I knew all about the original seven astronauts. While they collected baseball cards, I collected cards with satellites on them (*Nimbus, Echo, ISOS-I*). I ordered the *NASA Facts* publications from the Government Printing Office. For ten or fifteen cents you got the dream of space flight. I had a little floppy record of Kennedy's speech committing us to fly to the moon. It had come in *National Geographic*. I ran my own space program: I flew model rockets in competitions and was nationally ranked in the top twenty for a time. I had the history of the Space Race lined up in models all around my room. With my paper route money I bought a telescope and joined a group of amateur astronomers.

Anytime I was home during a launch, I watched it. I could imitate the staticky Mission Control transmissions. One of the Gemini astronauts had a son about my age who was just learning to ride his bicycle. Coverage of the family was part of each launch, as if the whole family and their pets were being shot into orbit. Our teacher would ask us to pray for the astronauts when they were circling the earth high above Cuba Hill.

I watched one "countdown" while lying on my back, astronaut-style, with my legs up on a hassock, trying to eat the "Space Food" I'd gotten for my birthday. (It tasted like freeze-dried Melba toast.)

The moon landing was the big event, maybe even bigger on Long Island. The LEM—the Lunar Excursion Module—was made on Long Island, and often starred in *Newsday* and *Life* magazine. The ungainly LEM was our hometown hero.

We went across the street to the Schwartzes' to watch the first steps on the moon. The lunar pictures were a play of shadows, but their TV made it worse. They had a black-and-white TV so fuzzy that Ozzie and Harriet looked like they were being beamed from the moon. At the crucial, epoch-making moment, with Neil Armstrong starting down the ladder to set foot on the Sea of Tranquility, Mrs. Schwartz left the room and returned with a hat she had just bought. She and my mother were discussing it—*a hat!* They were chattering away: *Isn't it nice! Yes, isn't it nice! It's a little different. Yes, don't you think so? I can wear it with my yellow dress, you know the one. . . .*

I leaned closer to the TV, practically fell into it, but I could hardly hear Mission Control.

Finally, I excused myself and ran across the street, back to our black-and-white TV—aware, as I crossed the street, that way, way above us men were on the moon. The space program did that; it lifted your sight.

I was twelve years old and I thought that I had seen the beginning— "the dawn of a new era." We'd be going to the planets soon and beyond. The moon landing was one of the biggest things ever in history. That's what I told a man I met in Macy's. I was looking at a big poster congratulating the astronauts. He came up and asked me what I thought about it all and I told him. He was wearing a suit and a tie and he really listened to what I said. The moon landing was the first really good news in a while. Everyone was talking about it. The moon was a celebrity that summer. Nineteen sixty-nine was a year so turbulent we had to leave earth to find a Sea of Tranquility.

The Sixties Happened Anyway

The trees grew up and the kids grew up and another war came along, one that wasn't a declared war but a "conflict" in official-speak—the Vietnam Conflict. Vietnam confounded the veterans. All of it: why we were there, why we didn't fight to win, why the kids wouldn't fight, why they did drugs and listened to "that music."

Despite their best efforts, the sixties happened anyway. They arrived in big shocks on the nightly news and locally, delivered by teenagers doing stupid things, like holding up a pack of cigarettes to a television camera. Lark, a new cigarette brand, advertised "Show us your Lark pack" with candid shots of men and women in the street holding up their Larks. One day the cameras rolled down Elwood Road and a high-school student, caught up in the excitement, waved his cigarette pack. I don't recall if this was broadcast, maybe it was, but soon the alarms were sounded: our teens are smoking! A big school district meeting was held. Parents stood up to say this has to stop.

The Lark incident was upstaged a few years later when a teacher approached two students who were smoking just off school grounds and discovered a "marijuana cigarette," in the words of the school district newsletter. More alarms, more meetings. An expert from the Police Department burned some hemp so that parents could learn to recognize the smell on clothes or coming from under closed bedroom doors.

The schools flew into a frenzy of drug education. I was in junior high school. I learned that marijuana was sometimes called "Mary Jane" and sometimes "reefer" and that it led to harder drugs and "antisocial behavior." It seemed that after one puff you could find yourself, in a few weeks, tying a hose around your arm and shooting "smack" in a flophouse. Or you could be derailed by taking "uppers" and "downers" that came in a rainbow of colors and had more nicknames than an old baseball team—just "go ask Alice when she's ten feet tall."

Everything was a drug. Some kids were sniffing Pam—the cooking spray—and some kids were sniffing glue. How many kids? No one I knew or heard about. It just made it difficult to buy glue to build model rockets, airplanes, and cars. You were presumed to be guilty.

The "marijuana cigarette" incident was in turn overshadowed by the protests to end the war. (Vietnam was *the* war now.) One morning in May 1971, when I was almost fourteen years old, the students at the high school joined a national day of protest. They sat down and refused to go to class. The bells rang and they refused to budge. The school principal threatened that this would go on their "permanent record." If they had already been admitted to college, that college would be notified. The students stood up and marched out of the school and down the road to the school district offices. They had broken the cardinal rule: children were not to be seen or heard. The strike leaders were rounded up and brought into the principal's office; parents were called.

I was in junior high school, far from the action, but the walkout was avidly debated, as it was at home among my parents' friends. The school district meeting that followed was anguished. Many parents wanted to know who put the kids up to this protest, as if their children couldn't watch the nightly news and see what was going on. They were looking for someone to blame.

The Angry Vet

He came to our junior high school to tell us about the war. He had been an art student in our school. He had great talent and in one quick hop became a highly paid illustrator in New York. Those languorous sketches of the women in the full-page Lord & Taylor ads in the *Times*? He drew those. He was a young man with a great career. He was drafted. Wounded, he came home unable to draw and paint. He was still in his twenties with his entire, reduced life ahead of him. All the teachers knew him, and they brought our Social Studies class to see him in the auditorium. He was on an anti-recruiting mission. He was telling us to wake up; we were going to Vietnam.

When the bell rang for the next class and we started to move, he fixed us in his gaze: *Punch the kid next to you. He'd be gone. Killed in battle.* I think this is what he said. Across all these years, I remember the intensity of his gaze, a laser shot at us. I think that he sat a little hunched over on the lip of the stage with his limp right arm in his lap—I'm not sure—but I remember that look in his eyes. His anger was white hot.

I heard that he killed himself. Finished the job.

~

One of those summers during the war, a man—a regular lawn-mower-pushing, nine-to-five family man—cracked and painted Clay Pitts Road in big letters: STOP THE WAR. People were enraged. Things were spiraling out of control: *you don't deface a county road.* He was facing jail time. This may have been after Kent State in May 1970, or it may have been the same summer that someone found LSD in the sugar containers at Adventureland, a small amusement park whose name was not meant as an ironic commentary on the American roller coaster ride of that decade.

Forty Miles II—Coming Home

The train platforms of Penn Station are the gates to the dream of sylvan peace. On these grimy platforms in the humid-on-humid air of the summer commute, ties are loosened and the workday ends with a push to grab a seat.

The father of a friend of ours told us this story. He worked in the city with a man who was going to quit his job any day, "quit the rat race." He talked eagerly of doing it. He was going to join a small company close to home. He thought the small company had great prospects. One evening he dropped dead right on the platform. Heart attack.

He suffered the emblematic commuters' death—his life literally commuted—in the original meaning of the word: shortened.

This story has been passed from father to son, a cautionary tale, like something that would have been in *Death of a Commuter* if Arthur

Miller had written it. The old ghost Ben returning to say: never die on a train platform, son.

Forty Miles III—The Commute between Today and Yesterday

One morning when I was in my twenties, our neighbor across the street gave me a lift to the train station. I was visiting my parents. It was very early and I was still sleepy and would have been happy to sit in a drowsy stupor, but he wanted to talk. He was still upset about the anti-war protests, which were more than a decade past. He wanted answers. I had been too young during the protest years, but I wore my hair long, so he must have thought I knew. This wasn't the first time I have been asked to explain protests that I had no part in.

Why did they destroy property? Why did they spit on the flag? he asked.

Where to start? I explained that they were trying to stop the great horrors the United States was committing in Vietnam. It was odd to be discussing this so quietly. I remember the anger, the complete miscommunication. A kid would be talking about how we were burning huts and bombing the jungle and an adult would answer: *Why don't you get a haircut?*

Our quieter discussion ended up in much the same place. But was it necessary to burn the flag? he asked. To wear a flag on the seat of your pants? There was no reconciling Veterans Island with the America on the nightly news.

This is a good country, he was saying. He had fought in a war. He had done his part; why couldn't these kids do their part? They had it very good.

And they did have it good, all those kids who were Little Leaguers just moments ago, who had sung *My country 'tis of thee, sweet land of liberty* morning after morning. Why did they spit on the flag?

To him they had destroyed the peace he had helped to win. They might as well have smashed his picture window and dug up his lawn.

They might as well have ridden rings around his house, wrecking the front and back and the side yards. You can't date it precisely, but somewhere in among all the protests, riots, and assassinations, in the smell of pot on their sons and daughters, Veterans Memorial Island came to an end in heartbreak.

There are many memorials to the world war the veterans won, but to me those slim side yards, those few feet between the houses, are the largest memorial. They started out as peace parks; block after block, mile after mile of watered, weeded, fertilized, and mowed peace parks.

THE RELIEF CANOES OF 1638

Downriver to the Future

I. "Welcome, Englishmen"

At the end of *The Great Gatsby*, Nick Carraway returns to West Egg one last time to pack and to visit his neighbor's house, Jay Gatsby's shuttered mansion, where once, he says, "there was music . . . through the summer nights. In his blue gardens men and girls came and went like moths among the whisperings and the champagne and the stars."

He walks down Gatsby's long lawn and sits on the beach looking across Long Island Sound in the dark, watching the glow of a ferryboat glide through the night. There are few lights to be seen; most of the big houses are closed for the season. He imagines the "old island here that flowered once for Dutch sailors' eyes—a fresh, green breast of the new world." In this moment of homecoming and farewell, Nick erases fifteen thousand years of history, erases the Mattinecock, Munsee, Mohegan, Pequot, and more than five hundred other Native American tribes. Gone. Never existed. Eden is empty.

We make the same mistake, the same false landfall every Thanksgiving. Our Thanksgiving story starts here with this myth of the New World. We set off telling our national story on the wrong foot and never recover.

～

The story most of us were taught in school about "The First Thanksgiving" is more false than true: in the fall of 1621, the Pilgrims, having survived their first year with the help of the local Indians, the

Wampanoags, sat down with their neighbors to a feast. It's a deceptive story, a trick achieved by the tight focus on one harvest celebration that was forgotten for more than two hundred years.

The Pilgrims were separatists, dissenters from the Church of England, twice exiled, first in Holland and then here in America. They had a rough crossing on the *Mayflower*. Her sister ship, the *Speedwell*, leaking badly, had to turn back only three hundred miles out to sea, adding more passengers to the overcrowded *Mayflower*. After more than two months at sea, they missed their destination by about two hundred miles, ending up off Cape Cod and not at the mouth of the Hudson River, where the king had permitted them to settle. They came ashore, stole from the Wampanoags' untended houses, corn reserves, and graves, and then wrote it all down.

In several locations they dug up corn that was stored in baskets and a kettle. They found more than they could carry. "So we took all the ears, and put a good deal of the loose corn in the kettle for two men to bring away on a staff; besides, they that could put any into their pockets filled the same." The rest they buried again. "And sure it was God's good providence that we found this corn, for else we know not how we should have done," wrote the Pilgrims Edward Winslow and William Bradford.

They entered the Wampanoags' houses, taking the "best things." "In the houses we found wooden bowls, trays and dishes, earthen pots, handbaskets made of crabshells wrought together. . . . There was also baskets of sundry sorts, bigger and some lesser, finer and some coarser; some were curiously wrought with black and white in pretty works. . . . Some of the best things we took away with us." They vowed to pay for what they had stolen: "So soon as we can meet conveniently with them, we will give them full satisfaction." They also robbed a few graves, taking "sundry of the prettiest things away with us," and covering "the corpse up again." (As an opening act it's sickeningly predictive.)

They settled in the Wampanoag village of Patuxet, which they named

Plymouth, knowing it was not occupied (though the Wampanoags still returned there to fish). The cleared fields—"much corn ground" —were there for the taking. The Pilgrims, and the Puritans ten years after them, had not come to a "waste and howling wilderness," as they said. Over thousands of years the Wampanoags had cultivated a prosperous and bountiful land. Thriving villages called sachemships were connected by a network of trails that ran through the forest and fields. Along the trails they had dug small holes about a foot deep that were story-markers, reminders of the stories to be told at that spot. They grew corn, beans, squash, and melons, hunted deer and other animals, gathered acorns, berries, and roots, and fished by building weirs in the rivers and along the seacoast, where they also harvested crabs, oysters, scallops, and clams. With the many "gardens and corn fields . . . the greatness of the timber growing on them, the greatness of the fish . . . this is a most excellent place, both for health and fertility," wrote the English explorer John Smith in 1616, advertising the region to prospective investors and settlers.

The Pilgrims had arrived in late December, missing the crucial growing season, with many sick from the crossing. That first winter, forty-five of the Mayflower's one hundred and two passengers died. By spring only six or seven were well enough to work. The Wampanoags kept track of them from a distance and debated whether to greet them or to kill them. It would have been a simple matter to erase the Pilgrims from North America.

They had reason to be wary. The Pilgrims were not the first Europeans they had met. For more than one hundred years, explorers and fishing fleets had been making their way to New England. These meetings were marked by curiosity, trade, sporadic fighting, and slave-taking by the English and others. Nearly every encounter with the Europeans led to violence.

But the Wampanoags had been tested by the years they called "The Great Dying." An epidemic from 1616 to 1619, which may have been smallpox, had killed as many as nine out of ten of the coastal Indians.

"A whole village might have two survivors, and those two survivors were not just like any two people," says historian Jill Lepore. "They were two people who had seen everyone they know die miserable, wretched, painful—excruciatingly painful—deaths." The Pilgrims found fields of bones lying above ground.

"There hath, by God's visitation, reigned a wonderful plague, the utter destruction, devastation, and depopulation of that whole territory, so as there is not left any that do claim or challenge any kind of interest therein," said King James I, dismissing the thousands of Indians who remained. God had cleared the way for the English. Vacant land could be seized—*vacuum domicilium* in English law.

The Wampanoags, much depleted, were exposed to attack from their rivals to the south, the Narragansetts, who were spared from the epidemic. They were looking for allies. The sachem the English called Massasoit decided to reach out to the Pilgrims. (His name was Ousamequin. Massasoit is an honorific meaning roughly the "highest chief who speaks on behalf" or Great Sachem.)

Massasoit called on Samoset, an Abenaki sagamore (a subordinate chief) who was a skilled negotiator. He walked out of the forest and said "Welcome, Englishmen." He had learned some English from the fishermen he had met where he lived on the Maine coast. That welcome is always in the stories of the First Thanksgiving.

With Samoset saying "Welcome, Englishmen," the Wampanoags walk into European history, into time as we keep it. They teach these Englishmen about planting corn and fishing, supply them with corn for years, and join them to celebrate the harvest. They sign a peace treaty. As the Thanksgiving story has been told, the Wampanoags live in the fog of prehistory. The English define them by what they don't have—no guns, no metal axes or metal cookware of their own making, no church, no written history. It's a view that persisted: "He built no cities, no ships, no churches, no schoolhouses," said a school textbook from 1880. "If he had any ideas of a Supreme Being they were vague and degraded."

Through the years, the Thanksgiving story has been presented as an endorsement by the Indians—"Oh white people, happy to see you. Here's a continent: Take it when you want—take all you want." In this story the Wampanoags exist only to ratify the Englishmen's arrival. They have no history of their own. The Indians are bit players in the epic story of bringing Christ to the "New World." Just that phrase— New World—erases them. They welcome the Pilgrims, teach them to feed themselves, and exit the story.

The Pilgrims' Thanksgiving—the one we're told is the First Thanksgiving—was not truly a thanksgiving. A true Pilgrim thanksgiving was about worship. Days of prayer were held to thank God for his mercy, for his evident acts of blessing his people with good crops or by ending a drought. Thanksgiving was a Christian holy day; non-Christians—heathens—were excluded. The opposite, days of humiliation or "Fast Days," were observed in day-long prayer to atone for sins and appease God's wrath. Days of thanks and self-mortification were called when the occasion demanded; they were not set on the calendar.

There was a feast with the Wampanoags outnumbering the English (not just a few standing solemnly to one side, as is usually shown in old paintings and prints). Massasoit arrived with ninety men; there were fifty-three Pilgrims. They stayed three days, dining on wild game (ducks, geese, and possibly wild turkey—abundant but hard to hunt with muskets), seafood (shellfish and eels, which were plentiful), and dishes made from Indian cornmeal. In thanks for the hospitality, Massasoit's men shot five deer, "which they bestowed on our governor, and upon the captain and others." In England, only the royalty and noblemen ate venison taken from the king's deer parks. There were "entertainments"—songs, possibly dancing, military drills and shooting muskets, competitions of speed and strength, and maybe games of chance, which the Wampanoags loved. This was a harvest celebration, a time of plenty coming after much hardship and death. It actually sounds like a good time, but nothing historic. The Pilgrims didn't rise after dinner to proclaim: Let the fourth Thursday in November be set aside forevermore for a day to give thanks (and for everyone to crowd roads and airports, have parades with big balloons of cartoon cats and dogs, watch football on big screen TVs, line up for Black Friday sales of big screen TVs, and eat turkey leftovers for weeks).

This feast was noted in just a few lines in an account of the Pilgrims' first months, *Mourt's Relation*. It was then forgotten for almost 220 years until it was reprinted in 1841 with a footnote by a Unitarian minister, saying, "This was the first Thanksgiving, the harvest festival of New England"—one of the most influential footnotes ever written.

The Pilgrims didn't set the myth of the First Thanksgiving in motion; they were recruited for this tale, enlisted in the late 1800s to help make immigrant children into WASP-like Americans. The Pilgrims were everyone's forefathers, no matter if a child's parents spoke Polish or Russian or Italian at home. America was the *Sweet land of liberty . . . . Land where my fathers died, Land of the pilgrims' pride.* This song, "America (My Country 'Tis of Thee)," sung to the tune of "God Save the Queen," was one of the unofficial national anthems until "The Star-Spangled Banner" was adopted in 1931.

The Pilgrims were portrayed as models of virtue, piety, and hard work, good Christians who were at peace with the Indians. The story became a group of images—memes—tall hats with buckles, all-black clothes, fat blunderbuss guns, Indians often in Plains Indian dress. (All wrong: no black clothes, no buckled hats, no wide-mouthed blunderbusses but muskets instead, and Wampanoags did not dress like Lakota Sioux. Also, this group of separatists, though likened to pilgrims on a pilgrimage, did not call themselves Pilgrims.)

This whole story is like the faded Thanksgiving classroom decorations taken out every year. It's a cartoon tale, a parade of big balloons we march down Broadway on the fourth Thursday of November, a parade of wrong ideas told to children.

~

The tale of the First Thanksgiving puts a frame around one harvest celebration. It presents amity, while hiding distrust, intrigue, and warfare. The story is framed to exclude what we don't want to admit about the country's founding.

There was peace, but it was an uneasy peace. Just a year after that harvest dinner, Miles Standish and his men knifed to death Pecksuot and Wituwamat and five other Massachusetts Indians they believed were conspiring to attack Plymouth. Standish and his men invited them to a feast and then assassinated them with their own knives. The Pilgrims were now called Wotowequenage—cutthroats.

"The early history of the Wampanoags and Plymouth took place against this dark background of mourning, suspicion, desperation, and fear. It's the most basic element missing from the Thanksgiving myth," says historian David J. Silverman.

The uneasy peace between the natives and the English held for more than a decade, until the Puritans of the Bay Colony, expanding to found new towns along the Connecticut River, ran into the Pequots, who had ambitions to dominate the neighboring tribes and control the fur and wampum trade with the Dutch. The Puritans, allied with the Narragansetts and Mohegans, fought the Pequot War in 1636 and 1637. The English way of war—fierce, total war without mercy—stunned the Pequots and the Puritans' Indian allies. At Mystic, Connecticut, on May 26, 1637, Captain John Mason and his men set a fort on fire, killing between four and seven hundred women and children including perhaps one hundred fifty Pequot warriors, in less than an hour. Those racing out of the fire were slain by the sword, "some hewed to pieces," or shot in a volley of musket fire so wild that some Narragansetts were also killed. Only fourteen Pequots survived. The Narragansetts fled, disgusted with their allies. This was the first massacre of native people in North America. It's a horrific attack; the Indians took note. The English expanded and were largely unchallenged for nearly forty years. The Pequots were crushed. They were disbanded, forbidden to live in their former territory, forbidden to call themselves Pequots "to cut off the remembrance of them from the earth," said Captain Mason. They were taken captive by neighboring tribes or enslaved and sent to the Caribbean. The Puritans celebrated with a day of Thanksgiving and praise. This was the Connecticut Colony's first Thanksgiving.

The English justified the massacre as a victory over Satan. "It was a fearful sight to see them thus frying in the fire, and the streams of blood quenching the same, and horrible was the stink; but the victory seemed a sweet sacrifice . . . to God," said William Bradford, the governor of the Plymouth Colony. "In a little more than *one hour*, five or six hundred of these barbarians were dismissed from a world that was *burdened* with them," said the Puritan minister Cotton Mather. When other Pequots arrived "to see the ashes of their *friends* mingled with the ashes at the fort, and the bodies of so many of their countrymen terribly *barbikew'd*, where the English had been doing a good morning's work, they howled, they roared, they stamped, they tore their hair . . . and were the pictures of so many devils in desperation."

The Pequot War was a forecast. The war's veterans applied the tactics to other native people seven years later, burning a village of five hundred Munsee, gunning down the escapees. The English were pushing for more land; their population was growing faster than almost any other in the world. In the Great Migration, some twenty thousand Puritans poured into Massachusetts Bay from the 1620s to the 1640s, until there were nearly as many English as native people. They set up towns on rivers farther inland. To the Indians, the English looked like they were "swarming," says one historian. They were closing in on their allies, the Narragansetts, pressing in from three sides.

The Narragansett Chief Miantonomi had learned a lesson from the Pequot War, even as his people had benefited. He wanted native peoples to be allies standing together. We should unite as the English have, he said, "otherwise we shall be all gone shortly, for you know our fathers had plenty of deer and skins, our plains were full of deer, as also our woods, and of turkeys, and our coves full of fish and fowl. But these English having gotten our land, they with scythes cut down the grass, and with axes fell the trees; their cows and horses eat the grass, and their hogs spoil our clam banks, and we shall all be starved." He was captured in a battle with the Mohegans and executed.

~

Massasoit's diplomacy had ensured more than fifty years of peace between the Wampanoags and the Pilgrims, from 1621 to 1675, but the world was changing again and his sons knew this. The youngest son of the peacemaker, Metacom or King Philip, would wage the most costly war, per capita, ever fought in America.

"The English who came first to this country were but a handful of people, forlorn, poor and distressed," Philip, now a sachem, explained to a Rhode Island official who wanted to keep the peace. "My father was then sachem. He relieved their distress in the most kind and hospitable manner. He gave them land to plant and build upon . . . they flourished and increased. By various means they got possession of a great part of his territory. But he still remained their friend till he died. My elder brother became sachem. . . . He was seized and confined and thereby thrown into illness and died. Soon after I became sachem they disarmed all my people. . . . Their land was taken. But a small part of the dominion of my ancestors remains. I am determined not to live until I have no country." The English cutthroats were ungrateful; they kept taking more land.

Philip led an uprising against the English colonies in Massachusetts, Rhode Island, and parts of Connecticut and Maine. It was a short, ferocious war. He struck on June 24, 1675, and in the following months, Indians attacked more than thirty towns, destroying some completely. So many settlers evacuated the Connecticut River Valley that the militia commander forbade anyone else to leave. By February 1676, Philip and his allies were striking within ten miles of Boston and it looked as if the English would have to retreat to a few fortified seacoast towns.

The colonists were terrified, fearing a united Indian uprising. But native people were divided. Some of the Wampanoags, Nipmucs, and Pocumtucks joined with Philip. The Wampanoags on Cape Cod stayed outside the fight. At the start, the powerful Narragansetts were neutral, harboring Wampanoag refugees, until the English and Mohegans attacked. The colonists did not start winning the war until they adopted Indian tactics and were tipped off by their native allies about King Philip's whereabouts.

The Indians and English lived close. They had lived with each other in trust and mistrust, trade and treaty, intermarriage and taboo, war and peace, tolerance and intolerance. Their worlds were interwoven in ways that are hard to know today. King Philip's War was a civil war, says one historian; it was a holy war against barbarians, "the perfect children of the devil," as one Puritan minister wrote. The Indians were too much with them, were too close, a daily reminder that threatened the Puritans, who believed they had been chosen to found an "English Israel" on "land the Lord God of Our Fathers hath given us for rightful possession." They feared becoming Indians. These two threads run through the contemporary accounts of the war: the proximity of these two worlds and the Puritans' vehemence. ("These Heathens being like Wolves and other Beasts of Prey, that commonly do their Mischiefs in the Night, or by Stealth, durst not come out of the Woods and Swamps, where they lay skulking in small Companies," is a typical passage of a history published toward the war's end.)

In fourteen months, the war was over. The English had begun to attack the Indians' food supplies and camps. "If Philip's forces had been better supplied and had not had to fight three wars at once— one with the English, one with their Pequot, Mohegan, and Christian Indian allies, and one with the Mohawks—the colonists might well have lost everything. And they knew it," says historian Jill Lepore.

King Philip was killed in August 1676, shot by an Indian guide who had led Captain Benjamin Church and his troops to a swamp near his home in Mount Hope, Rhode Island. Church declared Philip "a doleful, great, naked, dirty beast" and ordered Philip to be quartered and hung from the trees. "For as much as he has caused many a Pilgrim to lie above ground, unburied, to rot, not one of his bones shall be buried," Church said. He marched to Plymouth with Philip's head. His arrival on August 17 was marked as a day of thanksgiving, a declared day of prayer. They put King Philip's head on a tall pole and left it there for decades.

~

The war had laid waste to New England. The Indians who had allied against the English suffered the worst casualties—losing the greatest proportion of their population—of any war fought on American territory. Nearly 70 percent of the Wampanoag, Nipmuc, Niantic, and Narragansett people in southeastern New England were killed, fled as refugees, or were forced into servitude in English households or sold into slavery in the Caribbean. King Philip's nine-year-old son was sold as a slave. At the war's end there were public executions of Indians in Boston. But the Indians who had helped the English were punished too: they lost land and liberty. Before the war, one in four New Englanders was an Indian. After their defeat, and increasing English immigration, Indians were only one-tenth of the total population and their political power was marginal.

The colonists suffered for a century: one in sixteen men of military age was killed, half of the towns were ruined, and the economy was hobbled. "Per-capita incomes in New England did not recover their 1675 levels until 1775. They did not exceed the pre-1676 norm until after 1815," says historian Stephen Saunders Webb. The population did increase tenfold, but "these children of the Puritans, however, started from scratch and 'scratch' was not what it had been before 1676. A large share of the capital of the Puritan fathers, the investments of their all by the colonizing generations of New England, had been consumed in the fires of King Philip's War." New England would be dependent on England for a century. After the war, English and Irish churches sent ships with relief aid.

~

These three Thanksgivings—the first harvest celebration in 1621, the rejoicing over the slaughter of the Pequots in 1637, and King Philip's head presiding over a day of thanks in 1676—can be taken as the trajectory of our arrival in the New World. This was how the Europeans really encountered "a fresh, green breast of a new world." In just fifty years, the English and the natives went from a wary alliance and a friendly feast to a massacre and a bloody war.

At the center of our Thanksgiving is a story of ingratitude, of taking, not giving. The story of Thanksgiving should not be told without King Philip's War. But a story that ends "And then we killed them, and sold them into slavery" is not the making of a happy holiday.

II: "Thanks, But No Thanks"

The Thanksgiving Day we know was created to save the Union. Our great day of gratitude was born in strife. In 1863, President Lincoln proclaimed a national "day of Thanksgiving and Praise" at the urging of a magazine editor who was a household name. Sarah Josepha Hale led a seventeen-year-long campaign for the holiday in *Godey's Lady's Book*, which was the most widely read magazine in the country. In the midst of the Civil War, the president asked Americans to "fervently implore" the almighty to "heal the wounds of the nation, and to restore . . . the full enjoyment of peace, harmony, tranquility, and union."

Hale loved the Union as she loved her family. She was thirty-four years old with four children and a fifth due within weeks when her husband David died. He was a small-town lawyer in Newport, New Hampshire, a much-admired leading man of the community. She would wear black the rest of her long life. With his death, his family faced penury. In Hale's time it was common to break up a widow's family, sending children off to aunts and uncles and others, like the Shakers, who would take in children. Hale tried to keep her family together, supporting herself at first by sewing, which she found wearying, and later, with some local backers, by writing. She wrote herself out of poverty with her first novel, *Northwood*, published in 1827, and was asked to edit a women's magazine in Boston. There she created the modern women's magazine. When Louis Godey acquired the magazine, he was acquiring her talent. They would work together for forty years.

Even as she lived in cities, advising her readers on good taste, manners, and morals, in *Godey's* and in fifty books, Hale remained a small-town New England girl who was born with the new country, a year before George Washington took office. Her parents revered Washington. Her father, who had fought in the Revolution and was seriously wounded, thought Washington was infallible. Her mother taught her Washington's "Rules of Civility and Decent Behavior." Washington was one of the first words she learned to say.

Her loyalty to "the Father of His Country" and to the Union is what lay behind her untiring campaign for a national day of Thanksgiving— the same day in every state: all Americans united in gratitude. If Americans could look at what unites them, she believed, they would see they were more than northerners and southerners: "No discord would be possible." She had asked Lincoln to see Thanksgiving as a "National and Fixed Union Festival." In one of her many editorials, "Our Thanksgiving Union," she wrote in 1859: "If every state would join in Union Thanksgiving on the 24th of this month, would it not be a renewed pledge of love and loyalty to the Constitution of the United States which guarantees peace, prosperity, progress and perpetuity to our great Republic?"

Washington had proclaimed a "day of thanksgiving and prayer" shortly after taking office in 1789, a proclamation that Hale frequently quoted. President Adams continued the practice, but Jefferson refused, believing that a call for prayer and reflection violated the separation of church and state. Madison's proclamation in 1815 ended the tradition. After that, Thanksgiving was observed primarily on different days among the six New England states, any time from October to January. The young country's one great holiday was the Fourth of July.

"We have too few holidays," Hale wrote. "There is a deep moral influence in these periodical seasons of rejoicing, in which whole communities participate. They bring out . . . the best sympathies in our natures." She wrote thousands of letters to politicians and influential people, pleading her case, and she sent petitions to five presidents. Each year, in the magazine, she published a running tally of states that had adopted the fourth Thursday. By 1860, Hale had won over all but three states and eight territories before the Civil War tore her day of concord apart. The Confederacy went its own way, declaring days of thanksgiving after victories at the First and Second Battle of Bull Run.

Thanksgiving was the mythic past that would consecrate the present; it was a shared ceremonial history that would bind the states. In the nineteenth century, some thought the railroad would be the "iron bands" to unite the nation; some thought it was Protestant Christian belief and a founding story beginning in New England or Virginia. Before the Civil War, Americans spoke of their country in the plural, says historian Shelby Foote. They said, the United States *are*. After the war, they said the United States *is*. *E. pluribus unum*—out of many, one—has been elusive since thirteen colonies striving to be one nation adopted the motto.

As Hale tells the Thanksgiving story, the Pilgrims receive scant mention, and there are no Indians. In her novel *Northwood*, she devotes a chapter to Thanksgiving. The family goes to church in the morning and returns to an improbably large meal of roast turkey, pork leg, mutton joint, beef sirloin, chicken pie, goose, a pair of ducklings, bowls of gravy, vegetables, pickles, preserves, butter, bread, plum pudding, custards, "pies of every name and description ever known in Yankee land," cakes, sweetmeats, fruit, currant wine, cider, ginger beer, and an "innovation"—tea and coffee. Thanksgiving is an elaborately prepared stage to celebrate domestic simplicity—family gathered in sight of God, committed to acts of charity, released from the struggles of making a living. An English visitor is conveniently on hand for the head of the household to explain this "tribute of gratitude to God." Once, the Pilgrims in Boston were starving, he is told. They declared a day of fasting, but that day a ship arrived from England "laden with provisions, and so the fast was changed into a Thanksgiving." Her Pilgrims, relocated to Boston, inhabit a *vacuum domicilium*.

Thanksgiving wasn't Hale's only campaign, but it's representative. She was a crusading traditionalist. She fought for women's education, better wages and working conditions, better treatment of children, started the first day nursery, campaigned to save Mount Vernon, and raised money to finish the Bunker Hill Monument. She established the Seaman's Aid Society and worked to get women into medical schools. She carved out a big place for herself in a man's world and sought the same for her readers, but she was a conservative reformer—she was against slavery, but opposed abolition because it would burn down the temple, as she said, to save the temple. She proposed that church congregations take up collections to buy slaves their freedom. She was a feminist who didn't support suffrage and the women's rights movement. She told her readers that taking part in politics was "unfeminine" and that a good education was best used for "the most important vocation on earth . . . that of the Christian mother in the nursery." The women's rights movement responded by passing an admiring resolution: "While guarding with jealous care women's real rights and highest culture she so mingled in her daily life and writings the spirit of progress with true conservatism that she never compromised true womanly nature." They accepted her version of feminism.

Hale wanted to stop time, to invent a tradition that would be a still point in a nation heading toward Civil War. Thanksgiving fulfills historian Eric Hobsbawm's criteria for an "invented tradition"—it establishes or symbolizes "social cohesion" (one day of thanks for all); legitimizes institutions (the Union, the Constitution); and instills "beliefs . . . and conventions of behavior" (in turkey, stuffing, and pumpkin pie, we trust).

But as her campaign succeeded, and the nation paused on the fourth Thursday of November, the holiday changed. People stopped going to church in the morning. Other activities crowded out piety. For some it became a day of mischief and misrule. In New York City, men began celebrating in the morning with free drinks in the downtown taverns. At the call of a horn, costumed revelers would empty out into the streets for an unruly parade of "fantastics," some masked, some in drag, on horseback and in carts, blowing horns into the faces of female spectators. They would arrive in Central Park to picnic, drink, fight, and dance until early morning. These rowdy marches were eventually discouraged and diffused, to be reborn in the 1920s as the department store parade announcing the arrival of Santa. Football was also on the scene early, with the first college game in 1876, as an occasion for betting.

Thanksgiving, it turns out, was invented many times, layers adding to layers, but with the lurching movement of bumper cars in an amusement park, ideas colliding: Pilgrims and Sarah Josepha Hale (both dressed in black) and drunken mischief and football and shopping and laments that the holiday is being corrupted. Thanksgiving is the perfect American tradition—it seems eternal but it's malleable. "Radical impermanence as an enduring tradition," as Philip Roth said. Change is our tradition.

But above all, the Pilgrims presided, accessorized with their helpful friends, the Indians. The Pilgrims became the *ur*-immigrants in a nation of immigrants. They were the universal ancestor, honored along with Washington on his day and the Declaration of Independence on its day. And year after year, the Wampanoags became a generic sort-of Plains Indian, once savage or once noble, but doomed to vanish. And it all got to be too much, too hurtful, for the native people who were still very much here.

~

In 1970, the cardboard Pilgrims sailed into trouble. Massachusetts was planning a big event to commemorate the 350th anniversary of the Pilgrims' landing. They invited Frank James, a Wampanoag teacher from Cape Cod, to speak at the governor's banquet. These were enlightened times; the natives were allowed a place at the table. James was from Martha's Vineyard—Aquinnah to the Wampanoags, who had lived there for twelve thousand years. At age fourteen he had taken the name of the sachem Wamsutta, King Philip's brother, who some Wampanoags thought had been poisoned by the English. James wasn't going to offer a toast to the Pilgrims. He sent a draft of his speech to the state's commerce department at the department's request. They rejected it and handed him the speech they wanted him to read, one they had written about how the Pilgrims and Indians had lived together happily. He refused. They sent someone to his house to rewrite his speech with him. He again refused and withdrew two days before the banquet.

He gave his speech on Thanksgiving at a protest up on Cole's Hill by the statue of Massasoit, overlooking Plymouth Rock. He called for a new Thanksgiving tradition, a "National Day of Mourning," taking his cue from the Pequot preacher William Apess. In his *Eulogy on King Philip*, published in 1836, Apess called the Pilgrims' arrival and the Fourth of July "days of mourning and not joy."

Addressing a gathering of about two hundred, a mix of Indians from twenty-five tribes and tourists drawn away from the official celebration, Wamsutta Frank James said:

"It is with mixed emotion that I stand here to share my thoughts. This is a time of celebration for you—celebrating an anniversary of a beginning for the white man in America. A time of looking back, of reflection. It is with a heavy heart that I look back upon what happened to my People. Even before the Pilgrims landed it was common practice for explorers to capture Indians, take them to Europe and sell them as slaves for 220 shillings apiece. The Pilgrims had hardly explored the shores of Cape Cod for four days before they had robbed the graves of my ancestors and stolen their corn and beans," he said, referring to *Mourt's Relation*. Massasoit knew of these crimes, but still reached out to the Pilgrims. "This action by Massasoit was perhaps our biggest mistake. We, the Wampanoag, welcomed you, the white man, with open arms, little knowing that it was the beginning of the end; that before fifty years were to pass, the Wampanoag would no longer be a free people. . . .

"What has happened cannot be changed, but today we must work towards a more humane America, a more Indian America, where men and nature once again are important; where the Indian values of honor, truth, and brotherhood prevail. You the white man are celebrating an anniversary. We the Wampanoags will help you celebrate in the concept of a beginning. It was the beginning of a new life for the Pilgrims. Now, 350 years later it is a beginning of a new determination for the original American: the American Indian."

Massasoit's statue has stood here silent for many years, he said. We have been silent too long. "Our spirit refuses to die."

His speech was upstaged by the Oglala Lakota activist Russell Means and the radical members of AIM, the American Indian Movement, who were part of the occupation of Alcatraz Island and would go on to the bloody standoff at Wounded Knee. "Listen. Listen to us, white men. Plymouth Rock is red. Red with our blood," Means declared. It is time to seize the replica of the *Mayflower* in the harbor as a "symbolic gesture to reclaim our rights in this country," he said. They raced downhill, stopping to pour sand on Plymouth Rock, and next stormed the *Mayflower II*, tossing a mannequin of the captain and a cannon overboard, and climbing the rigging to tear off English flags before the police chased them from the ship.

The protestors then marched, drumming and singing, to Plimoth Plantation, a recreation of the Pilgrim village, where Means met up with another AIM leader, Dennis Banks. They arrived as the museum was reenacting a traditional Thanksgiving dinner. The make-believe Pilgrims invited the real Indians to join them. "In the middle of the welcoming speech by the 'Pilgrim Fathers,' Dennis suddenly stood up at the head of the table, yelled, 'We're not going to eat this shit!' and upended the table," recalled Means. "The rest of us started to yell and turn over the other tables." Costumed Pilgrims were screaming, racing to get away. "We Indians were hollering and whooping." They grabbed four cooked turkeys and left. Later that night, some of the AIM crew painted Plymouth Rock red. This was not the protest James had in mind. The "national Indians," he said, had gone too far. He did not want to answer a violent history with more violence.

The National Day of Mourning became a tradition. Over the years, protesters confronted the town's "Pilgrims' Progress"—townspeople dressed as Pilgrims on their way to church. Some years there were scuffles. In 1997, the police pepper-sprayed the protestors and arrested them, charging them with disorderly conduct and riotous assembly. It was part of that year's Thanksgiving Day news highlight reel: Garfield floating down Broadway in Macy's parade, the Detroit Lions mauling the Chicago Bears, and the police beating up native people in a place that called itself "America's Hometown."

The protestors took Plymouth to court for police brutality. The town dropped its charges, and as part of a settlement, they paid for two monuments as witness to the Wampanoags' history. One plaque says, in part: "Many Native Americans do not celebrate the arrival of the Pilgrims and other European settlers. To them, Thanksgiving Day is a reminder of the genocide of millions of their people, the theft of their lands, and the relentless assault on their culture. Participants in a National Day of Mourning honor Native ancestors and the struggles of Native peoples to survive today."

Thanksgiving is a sad season for many Indians. All around them white people are rejoicing in a society built on their destruction. They are dressing up their children as little Pocahontases and Squantos for their school's Thanksgiving pageant. "We don't count in the everyday life of America. I think that perception has to change," says Linda Coombs, a Wampanoag who for years was the associate director of the Wampanoag Indigenous Program at Plimoth Plantation. (The museum has since changed its name to Plimoth Patuxet to better reflect native history.) The program has worked heroically to correct the muddled story. At Hobbamock's Homesite at Plimoth, some of the Wampanoags paint their faces black in mourning to greet visitors during Thanksgiving week. They want to start a discussion; they want questions. If there were a medal for Speaking Truth to White People it should be awarded to the Wampanoag Indigenous Program. (Common visitor's question: "Weren't you glad when the Pilgrims came?" Answer: "No," says Coombs. "We had lived for ten or twelve thousand years, by the archeological record, with the world as our creator had made it. And then in less than four hundred years we're at the brink of destruction with our 'advanced' technological and industrial society.") As the title of a Wampanoag Indigenous Program that I attended years ago put it, "Thanks, But No Thanks."

The thanks in our holiday is nearly invisible. Gratitude is missing from our Thanksgiving stories. "Gratitude is the most powerful Thanksgiving story from my perspective as a Wampanoag," says Ramona Peters, an artist and the founder of the Native Land Conservancy. Elementary school teachers should forget the myth and talk about being thankful, she says. "We can all be proud that our country has a national holiday centered upon simply being thankful. . . . When young children grasp gratitude in a real way, beyond ritual, our country will be greater." Buried under the collapsed myth is the impulse to celebrate peace, gratitude, and generosity.

III. A Forgotten Act of Generosity

In an unending season of hate and smash-mouth politics, when America was coming to seem like the ending of *The Lord of the Flies*—the island on fire, the children in vicious pursuit of each other—I longed for generosity. I wanted to find generous people, to find a more generous spirit within myself. I wanted to break free from Nick Carraway's blindness-inducing New World, from the Pilgrim's greed in *Mourt's Relation*, and from Sarah Hale's overstuffed Union Thanksgiving. Let's give 1621 a rest. Let's separate from the separatists and move 130 miles inland and seventeen years later to where the Pocumtucks lived up the Connecticut River from the Puritans. Thanksgiving is a layered, changing holiday, so let's change it.

In 1638, the year after the Pequots were massacred, the frontier outposts of Hartford and Windsor, Connecticut, were facing starvation. The Pequot War had disrupted farming, and the hard winter that followed, with as much as three feet of snow on the ground into early April, had delayed planting. The General Court ordered William Pynchon to buy five hundred bushels of corn from the Indians at a set price. The wealthy Pynchon was one of the founders of the Massachusetts Bay Company and the colony's treasurer. He moved inland to found Springfield and was the leading investor in the place he named after his English village. He was the new town's only merchant and only Indian trader. He and his son John held the legal monopoly to the valuable fur trade in the valley. William was also a savvy trader, charging a 20 percent markup for each bushel of corn he sold to his neighbors. He built a gristmill and a warehouse to store corn, grain, meat, and furs to ship to Boston and then on to London or the Caribbean. The Pynchons owned Springfield's best land; a third of the town's farmers leased land from them. John financed the new towns in the valley, determining when and where they would be settled.

William was in charge of administering justice. He was an elected magistrate, and served in the Massachusetts General Court when that colony took charge of Springfield. "For nearly a decade and a half, Pynchon was the only official contact between the executive, legislative and judicial branches of the colonial administration and this frontier community," writes historian Peter Thomas. "If the government acted at all, it acted through William Pynchon." The Pynchon family dominated life in their stretch of the "Great River," from the founding of Springfield in 1636 to the century's end.

William knew it would be hard to buy corn; he did not want to take on the assignment. The Indians nearby refused to sell. The Puritans had set the price too low. The Indians had received a higher price the previous year, when corn was plentiful.

He paddled thirty-five miles upriver to meet with the Pocumtucks. They lived in a small, fertile valley between the Connecticut River and the Pocumtuck (now Deerfield) River. The Pocumtuck River would flood miles of flat cornfields, leaving rich river silt. The Anglican cleric William Morrell would later say that this valley was "a briefe of what may make man blest." The Pocumtucks were a prosperous, healthy people, thought to be an influential tribe, one of the "great Indians" in the estimation of the Dutch in New York. They had been observed sending warriors downriver and across Long Island Sound to fight the Indians on Eastern Long Island, a journey of at least 150 miles by canoe. The English treated the Pocumtucks with restraint and caution.

The Pocumtucks' crop was usually bountiful; they stored the surplus underground. When Pynchon arrived in 1638, they were willing to sell five hundred bushels at the low price of five shillings a bushel, a price all the other Indians had refused. They knew the corn was worth much more, and they knew the Puritans were in want. They were paid in an equivalent amount of wampum—twelve thousand strings of beads, each a foot long. The trade was a good way for the Pocumtucks to make allies, but the corn was also a gift. The Pocumtucks helped the starving strangers.

Fifty canoes loaded with five hundred bushels of corn came down the river. At the sight of this "corn fleet," as it was called in one local history, the Puritans must have rejoiced or given thanks. They said, these Indians are our worthy neighbors. We'll respect their ways and learn from them. We'll not hunt on their lands. We'll honor our treaties with them.

No. Of course not—you know that. This was, after all, just a year after the massacre in Mystic. The Pocumtucks' gift may have long lived in the memories of the Puritans who had been rescued from famine, but it quickly exited written history.

Nowhere in the surviving accounts have I read about the gratitude of the English settlers. No Fast Day to pray and reflect, no day of Thanksgiving, no sermons honoring the Indians upriver, no spontaneous rejoicing. No thanks. Did I miss something? I asked the historian Peter Thomas. He has closely studied the Connecticut River Valley trading in the 1600s.

"Lack of a written record does not preclude the likelihood that thanks was given," Thomas says. "As far as I know, the documentary evidence for the very early years of settlement may well have not survived. What needs to be kept in mind, however, is that during the seventeenth century, in the Puritan mind, God was behind all actions and events. If there was a thanksgiving, it was to God who had provided for his children's survival in the wilderness. The deeds of men had little meaning."

What does remain is the doings of the Puritans. William Pynchon was charged with "unfaithful dealing in the trade of corn." He was tried for speculating, for buying the corn low and selling at a handsome profit in Hartford. In the "corn controversy," Pynchon, who once was everything to Springfield, was convicted of profiteering by the Connecticut General Court and fined forty bushels of corn. Old grudges seem to have come calling. Pynchon spent three years defending his reputation in court and in church. After publishing a religious tract critical of the Puritans, he was accused of heresy and returned to England a wealthy man.

Only twenty-six years later, the Pocumtucks were gone from their fertile valley, no longer a powerful tribe. They were on the losing end of a dispute with the Mohawks. Only a part of the story is known. The Mohawks—sometimes enemies, sometimes allies—sent a peace party to the Pocumtucks. On the return trip, the Mohawk sachem leading the party was killed. Months later the Mohawks, whom

William Pynchon had called "the terror of all Indians," returned to destroy the Pocumtucks' palisaded fort. The survivors scattered to live with other tribes.

Most likely the Puritans didn't thank the Pocumtucks for their gift in a starving time. Where's the monument in Hartford? The commemoration in Windsor? But these are not the most important questions. Three hundred and eighty years later, the question that I wish was at the table on Thanksgiving is: What will we do now in return?

I had first heard about the canoes more than twenty years ago, sitting in a quiet church in a town along the Connecticut River, just north of where the Pocumtucks had lived and died. Marge Bruchac, an Abenaki storyteller and scholar, was a guest delivering the morning's sermon two weeks before Thanksgiving. It was a homecoming of sorts: her ancestors had lived here and were still living here when the English, declaring the land abandoned, moved in. Her ancestors burned the English village four times.

On this morning, she told old stories about "that long river, that *Kwinitekw* River that flows from the north to the south," she said, using the Algonquian word that gave us Connecticut. She slowed as she pronounced it—*Kwin-eh-tek-wuh*—letting it sink in. In that quiet church, that old word seemed to stretch out. She talked about the Wampanoags welcoming the Pilgrims and how that generosity was twisted into the Thanksgiving story, which she summarized as: "Since the Indians helped us by sharing food with us, they wanted us to be here, and therefore they wanted us to take over. When in fact what we have been trying to do from the moment of first contact is talk about who we are, what we believe, how we lived in this place. And our generosity has often been our undoing. We had ancient traditions that said you always help the stranger. And you always care for them. And hopefully, you can figure out how to get along together." It did not work out that way.

The Pocumtucks helped the stranger. It's what we need now: someone to come down the river with a feast, with food and forgiveness. Someone to say, open your heart, take a holiday from your hate, let the hate-making machine—the broadcasts and tweets, the bloody fights in the street—let the hate-making machine rest. Accept today this gift. Love your enemy. Reload the canoes with gifts. Paddle back upriver with humility and thanks.

BIBLIOGRAPHY

Introduction: Seekers

Cross, Whitney R. *The Burned-Over District: The Social and Intellectual History of Enthusiastic Religion in Western New York, 1800–1850.* New York: Harper & Row, 1950.

Flint, Timothy. *Recollections of the Last Ten Years, Passed in Occasional Residences and Journeyings in the Valley of the Mississippi.* . . . Boston: Cummings, Hilliard, 1826.

Goodwillie, Christian. "Mummy Jum: The Shaker-Pilgrim Encounter of 1817–1818." *Communal Societies,* June 2014.

Ham, F. Gerald. "The Prophet and the Mummyjums: Isaac Bullard and the Vermont Pilgrims of 1817." *The Wisconsin Magazine of History,* Summer 1973.

The History of Warren County, Ohio. W. H. Beers & Company, 1882.

Howe, Daniel Walker. *What Hath God Wrought: The Transformation of America, 1815–1848.* Oxford: Oxford University Press, 2009.

Klingaman, William K., and Nicholas P. Klingaman. *The Year Without Summer: 1816.* New York: St. Martin's Press, 2013.

Ludlum, David M. *Social Ferment in Vermont 1791–1850.* New York: Columbia University Press, 1939.

Moore, R. Laurence. *In Search of White Crows: Spiritualism, Parapsychology, and American Culture.* Oxford: Oxford University Press, 1977.

Porte, Joel, ed. *Emerson in his Journals.* Cambridge, MA: Harvard University Press, 1982.

Stein, Stephen J. *Communities of Dissent: A History of Alternative Religions in America.* Oxford: Oxford University Press, 2003.

"No Good Is Ever a Failure"

Bervy, Elizabeth Gleason. "The Shakers of Canterbury: Their Agriculture and Their Machinery." *American Communal Societies Quarterly,* 4, no. 2 (April 2010).

Blinn, Henry C. *The Manifestation of Spiritualism among the Shakers 1837–1847*. United States: n.p., 1899.

Brewer, Priscilla J. *Shaker Communities, Shaker Lives*. Hanover, NH: University Press of New England, 1986.

"Bureau of Lecture & Concert Artists. Lawrence, Kansas. Talent Schedule. Attraction: Charles Thompson." January 1956–March 1956. Canterbury Shaker Village Archives.

Burns, Amy Stechler, and Ken Burns. *The Shakers: Hands to Work, Hearts to God*. New York: Aperture Foundation, 1987.

Burns, Ken. Interview with Melissa Laverack, April 1, 2014. https://www.youtube.com/watch?v=j6LO5NDTGzI

Burns, Ken, and Amy Stechler Burns. *The Shakers: Hands to Work, Hearts to God*. Film. 1984.

Canterbury Shaker Village Archives. Canterbury Collection: Addresses, Sermons, Essays, Other Writings.

———. Eldress Bertha Lindsay Archives Collection. Bertha Lindsay Office Collection.

———. The Darryl Charles Thompson Collection.

———. Recently donated and unfiled papers and letters from Charles "Bud" Thompson.

Court, Andy. "The Lives of the Last Shakers." *The Concord Monitor*, December 27, 1984.

Davenport, Tom, and Frank DeCola. *The Shakers*. Film. Folkstreams, 1974. http://www.folkstreams.net/film-detail.php?id=84

Emerson, Martha Mae. "Bud Thompson—No Place for Pickled Artifacts." *New Hampshire Profiles*, April 1975.

Fletcher, Brad. Interview with the author, July 14, 2019.

Fox, Renee. Interview with the author, July 8, 2019.

———. "Notes on Lecture by Charles 'Bud' Thompson, on meeting and living with the Shakers at Canterbury, twentieth century—11 January 2007." Canterbury Shaker Village Archives.

Gabor-Hotchkiss, Magda. "Brother Ricardo Belden Revisited." *American Communal Societies Quarterly*, 6, no. 1, (January 2012).

Garrett, Clarke. *Spirit Possession and Popular Religion*. Baltimore, MD: The Johns Hopkins University Press, 1987.

Garvin, James L. *Historic Structure and Cultural Landscape Report: Turning Mill Pond Dam and the Shaker Millpond System, Canterbury Shaker Village*. March 2018.

Goodwillie, Christian. "Light and Dark Sides of Spiritualism: The Eddy Brothers and the Shakers." *American Communal Societies Quarterly*, 9, no. 3 (July 2015).

Hill, Isaac. "A Chapter on the Shakers: Reprint." *American Communal Societies Quarterly*, 9, no. 2 (April 2015).

Hillinger, Charles. "Vanishing Shakers Leave Lasting Legacy." *The Los Angeles Times*, October 23, 1988.

King, Eldress Emma B. *A Shaker's Viewpoint*. Old Chatham, NY: Shaker Museum Foundation, 1957.

Kirkpatrick, Alberta MacMillan. Interview with Amy Stechler, 1999. Canterbury Shaker Village Archives.

Lamb, David. Interview with the author, May 9, 2019.

Lindsay, Eldress Bertha. Interview, January 29, 1978. Transcription by Mary Ann Sanborn. Canterbury Village Shaker Archives.

———. *Seasoned with Grace: My Generation of Shaker Cooking*. Woodstock, VT: The Countryman Press, 1987.

———. As told to Cable Neuhaus. "The Shakers Face Their Last Amen." *People*, March 2, 1987.

Lyford, James Otis. *History of the Town of Canterbury, New Hampshire, 1727–1912*. Concord, NH: The Rumford Press, 1912.

Marini, Stephen A. *Radical Sects of Revolutionary New England*. Cambridge, MA: Harvard University Press, 1982.

Marshall, Harold. "Arthur Nash: The Golden Rule." *The Master Mason*, June 1924.

Martin, David. "Serene Twilight of the Shakers." *Life*, March 17, 1967.

Merton, Thomas. *Seeking Paradise: The Spirit of the Shakers*. Edited with an introduction by Paul M. Pearson. New York: Orbis Books, 2003.

Morse, Flo. *The Shakers and the World's People*. Hanover, NH: University Press of New England, 1980.

National Historic Landmark Nomination, Canterbury Shaker Village. US Department of Interior, National Park Service, 1992.

New Hampshire Public Radio. "From the Archives: The Shakers." https://www.nhpr.org/post/archives-shakers#stream/0

O'Brien, Marcy. "A Simple Wish." *Yankee*, May 2001.

Pearson, Paul M., ed. *A Meeting of Angels: The Correspondence of Thomas Merton with Edward Deming & Faith Andrews*. Frankfort, KY: Broadstone Books, 2008.

Promery, Sally M. *Spiritual Spectacles: Vision and Image in Mid-19th Century Shakerism*. Bloomington, IN: Indiana University Press, 1993.

Randle, William, producer. *The Shaker Heritage: The American Culture Series*. Lectures recorded at Canterbury, NH, and Sabbathday Lake, ME, 1960–1961.

Sears, Clara Endicott, ed. *Gleanings from Old Shaker Journals*. Boston: Houghton Mifflin Company, 1916.

"The Shakers: A Strict and Utopian Way of Life has Almost Vanished." *Life*, March 21, 1949.

Sprigg, June. Interview with the author, May 2, 2019.

———. *Simple Gifts: A Memoir of a Shaker Village*. New York: Alfred A. Knopf, 1998.

Sprigg, June, and David Larkin. *Shaker: Life, Work, and Art*. New York: Harry N. Abrams, 2001.

Starbuck, David R. *Neither Plain nor Simple: New Perspectives on the Canterbury Shakers*. Hanover, NH: University Press of New England, 2004.

Starbuck, David R., and Scott T. Swank. *A Shaker Family Album: Photographs from the Collection of Canterbury Shaker Village*. Hanover, NH: University Press of New England, 1998.

Stein, Stephen J. *The Shaker Experience in America*. New Haven, CT: Yale University Press, 1992.

Stier, Maggie. Interview with the author, March 18, 2019.

Thompson, Charles "Bud." Interviews with the author, March 5, 2019; March 21, 2019; April 23, 2019.

Thompson, Darryl. "Forgotten Facts about a Founding." Unpublished paper, n.d.

———. Interview with the author, March 3, 2019.

Thompson, Darryl Charles. "The Story of Brother Ricardo's Song." *American Communal Societies Quarterly*, 5, no. 2 (April 2011).

Weiner, Eric. "Thin Places Where We Are Jolted Out of Old Ways of Seeing the World." *New York Times*, March 9, 2012.

Zanes, John. "In Search of the Sixth Sense." *New Hampshire Profiles*, March 1963.

"We Are Still in Eden"

Aponovich, Elizabeth. Interview with the author, April 13, 2004.

Aponovich, Elizabeth, and James Aponovich. Interviews with the author: January 14, 2010; February 11, 2010.

Aponovich, James. Interviews with the author: March 16, 2004; March

23, 2004; April 1, 2004; December 20, 2007; July 7, 2007; June 2, 2009; August 18, 2009; November 20, 2009.

Bedell, Rebecca B. "The Anatomy of Nature: Geology and Landscape Painting in the White Mountains." Lecture. New Hampshire Historical Society, February 11, 2007.

Bennett, Randall H. *The White Mountains: Alps of New England.* Columbia, SC: Arcadia Publishing, 2003.

Blaine, Marcia Schmidt. "Disaster's Lure: The Willey Slide." *Historical New Hampshire*, Spring 2020.

Bofinger, Paul. Interview with the author, June 12, 2018.

Bulkley, Peter B. "Identifying the White Mountain Tourist 1853–1854: Origin, Occupation, and Wealth as a Definition of the Early Hotel Trade." *Historical New Hampshire*, Summer 1980.

———. "Horace Fabyan, Founder of the White Mountain Grand Hotel." *Historical New Hampshire*, Summer 1975.

Campbell, Catherine H. "Albert Bierstadt and the White Mountains." *Archives of American Art Journal*, 1981.

———. "Two's Company: The Diaries of Thomas Cole and Henry Cheever Pratt on Their Walk Through Crawford Notch, 1828." *Historical New Hampshire*, Fall 1978.

Champney, Benjamin. *Sixty Years' Memories of Art and Artists.* United States: Wallace & Andrews, 1900.

Cole, Donald B. "The White Mountains in 1845: From the Journal of Benjamin Brown French." *Historical New Hampshire*, Winter 1989.

Cole, Thomas. "Essay on American Scenery." *American Monthly Magazine*, January 1836.

Conron, John. *American Picturesque.* Philadelphia: Pennsylvania State University Press, 2000.

Conroy, Rosemary G. and Richard Ober, eds. *People and Place: Society for the Protection of New Hampshire Forests: The First 100 Years.* Society for the Protection of New Hampshire Forests, 2001.

Coulter, Emilie, ed. *Passing Through: The Allure of the White Mountains.* Plymouth, NH: Museum of the White Mountains, Plymouth State University, 2013.

Crawford, Lucy. *The History of the White Mountains.* (1846). Portland, ME: B. Thurston & Company, 1886.

Dickerman, Mike, ed. *The White Mountain Reader.* Littleton, NH: Bondcliff Books, 2000.

Garvin, Donna-Belle, ed. "Beauty Caught and Kept: Benjamin Champney in the White Mountains." *Historical New Hampshire*, Fall/Winter 1996.

———. *Consuming Views: Art and Tourism in the White Mountains, 1850–1900*. New Hampshire Historical Society, 2006.

———. "A Suburb of Paradise: The White Mountains and the Visual Arts." *Historical New Hampshire*, Fall/Winter 1999.

Garvin, Donna-Belle, and James L. Garvin. *On the Road North of Boston: New Hampshire Taverns and Turnpikes, 1700–1900*. New Hampshire Historical Society, 1988.

Harris, John R., et al., eds. *Beyond the Notches: Stories of Place in New Hampshire's North Country*. Littleton, NH: Bondcliff Books in partnership with Monadnock Institute of Nature, Place and Culture at Franklin Pierce University, 2011.

Johnson, Christopher. *This Grand & Magnificent Place: The Wilderness Heritage of the White Mountains*. Hanover, NH: University of New Hampshire Press, 2006.

Kennedy, William. "God, Nature and Politics: The Ministry of Thomas Starr King." Paper for Unitarian Universalist history class, Starr King School for the Ministry. Berkeley, Calif. Spring 2004.

Keyes, Donald D., et al. *The White Mountains: Place and Perceptions*. Durham, NH: University Art Galleries, University of New Hampshire, 1980.

King, Thomas Starr. *The White Hills: Their Legends, Landscape, and Poetry*. Boston: Crosby, Nichols, and Company, 1860.

MacFarlane, Robert. *Mountains of the Mind*. New York: Random House, 2003.

Mansfield, Howard. "Life, Flowers, Air: The Journey from Garden to Canvas." In *James Aponovich: A Retrospective*. Manchester, NH: Currier Museum of Art, 2005.

McGrath, Robert L., and Barbara J. MacAdam. *"A Sweet Foretaste of Heaven": Artists in the White Mountains, 1830–1930*. Hanover, NH: Hood Museum of Art, Dartmouth College, 1988.

Miller, Angela. *The Empire of the Eye: Landscape Representation & American Cultural Politics, 1825–1875*. Ithaca, NY: Cornell University Press, 1993.

Nicolson, Marjorie Hope. *Mountain Gloom and Mountain Glory: The Development of the Aesthetics of the Infinite*. Ithaca, NY: Cornell University Press, 1959.

Noble, Louis L. *The Life and Works of Thomas Cole, N. A.* New York: Sheldon, Blakeman and Company, 1856.

Novak, Barbara. *Nature and Culture: American Landscape Painting 1825–1875.* Revised ed. Oxford: Oxford University Press, 1995.

Parker, Thomas B. *James Aponovich: An Abundant Life.* Exhibition catalog. New York: Hirschl & Adler, 2013.

Purchase, Eric. *Out of Nowhere: Disaster and Tourism in the White Mountains.* Baltimore, MD: The Johns Hopkins University Press, 1999.

Sears, John F. *Sacred Places: American Tourist Attractions in the Nineteenth Century.* Oxford: Oxford University Press, 1989.

Siegel, Nancy. "'I Never Had So Difficult a Picture to Paint': Albert Bierstadt's White Mountain Scenery and The Emerald Pool." *Nineteenth-Century Art Worldwide,* Autumn 2005.

Tolles, Byrant F., Jr. *The Grand Resort Hotels of the White Mountains: A Vanishing Architectural Legacy.* Boston: David R. Godine, 1998.

———. ed. "The Grand Resort Hotels and Tourism in the White Mountains." *Historical New Hampshire,* Spring/Summer 1995.

Truettner, William H., and Alan Wallach, eds. *Thomas Cole: Landscape into History.* New Haven, CT: Yale University Press/National Museum of American Art, 1994.

Ungar, Arliss. "Nature Writings: Words of the Rev. Thomas Starr King." Paper presented at the Unitarian Universalist Association General Assembly 2004. Starr King School for the Ministry, Berkeley, California.

Vogel, Charles O. "Artists in Residence in White Mountain Hotels." Lecture. New Hampshire Historical Society, March 4, 2007.

Waterman, Laura, and Guy Waterman. *Forest and Crag: A History of Hiking, Trail Blazing, and Adventure in the Northeast Mountains.* Boston: Appalachian Mountain Club, 1989.

Wemyss, Howie. Interview with the author, December 20, 2007.

Weschler, Lawrence. *Seeing Is Forgetting the Name of the Thing One Sees: A Life of Contemporary Artist Robert Irwin.* Berkeley, CA: University of California Press, 1982.

Lost Boundaries

Baldwin, James. *Collected Essays.* New York: The Library of America, 1998.

Bainbridge, John. "Little Magazine." *The New Yorker,* November 17, 1945.

Benaquist, Larry. "Notes to *Lost Boundaries* Reunion." *Lost Boundaries 40th Anniversary Reunion and Celebration* program, July 24, 1989.

Bogle, Donald. Interview with the author, July 1989.

———. *Toms, Coons, Mulattoes, Mammies, and Bucks. An Interpretative History of Blacks in American Films.* London: Bloomsbury Academic, 2016.

Bromley, Dorothy Dunbar. ("Special writer for *The New York Herald Tribune*.") Untitled article, n.d. *Lost Boundaries* scrapbook, series 2, box 3, Johnston Family Papers, Historical Society of Cheshire County.

Coleman, Lester. "Not 'Anti-Segregation': Censor Tells Why She Approved 'Home of the Brave' for Showing Here." *The Atlanta Constitution*, October 2, 1949.

Cripps, Thomas. *Making Movies Black.* Oxford: Oxford University Press, 1993.

Delton, Jennifer. "Before the White Negro: Sin and Salvation in *Kingsblood Royal*." *American Literary History,* Summer 2003.

DeSantis, Christopher, ed. *Langston Hughes and the Chicago Defender.* Champaign, IL: University of Illinois Press, 1995.

De Rochemont, Louis. *Lost Boundaries.* Film. Directed by Alfred L. Werker. RD-DR Corp., 1949.

Drenan, Sprague W. "'Lost Boundaries' Makes Deep Impression on Keene Audience." *The Keene Sentinel,* July 25, 1949.

Elliot Community Hospital Annual Reports, 1949–1950 and 1953–1954. Keene, New Hampshire.

Ellison, Ralph. *Shadow and Act.* Vintage International, 1995.

Ferrer, Mel. Interview with the author, July 1989.

Fielding, Raymond. *The March of Time, 1935–1951.* Oxford: Oxford University Press, 1978.

Gates, Henry Louis, Jr. "Segregation in the Armed Forces during World War II." www.pbs.org.

———. "White Like Me," *The New Yorker,* June 10, 1996.

George Washington Noyes House. National Register of Historic Places Registration Form, August 5, 2016.

Granton, E. Fannie. "Lost Boundaries Medic, Wife." *Jet,* November 13, 1969.

Hobbs, Allyson. *A Chosen Exile: A History of Racial Passing in American Life.* Cambridge, MA: Harvard University Press, 2014.

Irving, Debbie. *Waking Up White.* Cambridge, MA: Elephant Room

Press, 2014.

Jefferson, Margo. *Negroland: A Memoir*. New York: Pantheon Books, 2015.

Johnston, Albert. Correspondence with US Navy, and the Army Medical Corps, Johnston scrapbook, series 2, box 2, and series 1, box 1, folder 15, Johnston Family Papers, Historical Society of Cheshire County.

———. Speech to Camden NAACP, n.d. Personal papers, series 1, box 1, folder 5, Johnston Family papers, Historical Society of Cheshire County.

Johnston, Albert, Jr. Interview with the author, July 1989.

———. "Synopsis of Johnston Family Story," May 26, 1947. *Lost Boundaries* scrapbook, series 2, box 3, Johnston Family Papers, Historical Society of Cheshire County.

———. "Youth and the Race Problem." *The Survey*, June 1950.

Johnston, Thyra. Interview with the author, July 1989.

———. Letter to the author, August 17, 1989.

———. Letter to Louis de Rochemont, July 11, 1949. *Lost Boundaries* scrapbook, series 2, box 3, Johnston Family Papers, Historical Society of Cheshire County.

Kevles, Bettyann Holtzmann. *Naked to the Bone: Medical Imaging in the Twentieth Century*. New Brunswick, NJ: Rutgers University Press, 1997.

Kroeger, Brooke. *Passing: When People Can't Be Who They Are*. New York: Public Affairs, 2003.

Lewis, Sinclair. *Kingsblood Royal*. New York: Random House, 1947.

Lingeman, Richard. *Sinclair Lewis: Rebel from Main Street*. New York: Random House, 2002.

"Lost Boundaries Doctor Ousted, Charges Bias," *Jet*, June 25, 1953.

"Lost Boundaries. Exciting New Book Tells Case History of a Family That Passed for 20 Years." *Ebony*, May 1948.

"Lost Boundaries. New Film Records Chronicle of Negro Doctor Who 'Passed.'" *Ebony*, July 1949.

Louis de Rochemont Collection, Archive & Special Collections, Keene (NH) State College.

Lyons, Eugene. "Louis de Rochemont, Maverick of the Movies." *Reader's Digest*, July 1949.

Mansfield, Howard. "Prejudice and a Fraction of Success: The Albert

Johnston Story and a 'Lost Boundaries' Reunion," *Washington Post*, July 25, 1989.

McGehee, Margaret. "Disturbing the Peace: 'Lost Boundaries,' 'Pinky,' and Censorship in Atlanta, Georgia, 1949–1952." *Cinema Journal*, Autumn 2006.

Murdock, Clotye. "What Happened to the Lost Boundaries Family?" *Ebony*, August 1952.

New Hampshire Public Television, "Home to Keene: The Lost Boundaries Reunion." Film. 1989.

Oluo, Ijeoma. *So You Want to Talk About Race*. New York: Seal Press, 2018.

Pryor, Thomas M. "Hoeing His Own Row: The History of Louis de Rochemont and His New Film, 'Lost Boundaries.'" *New York Times*, June 26, 1949.

Schorer, Mark. *Sinclair Lewis: An American Life*. New York: McGraw-Hill Book Company, Inc., 1961.

Senna, Danzy. *Where Did You Sleep Last Night? A Personal History*. New York: Farrar, Straus & Giroux, 2009.

Smith, Judith E. *Visions of Belonging: Family Stories, Popular Culture, and Postwar Democracy, 1940–1960*. New York: Columbia University Press, 2004.

Strub, Whitney. "Black and White and Banned All Over: Race, Censorship and Obscenity in Postwar Memphis." *Journal of Social History*, Spring 2007.

"Superior Documentary." *Newsweek*, July 4, 1949.

"This Family was White for Twenty Years." *Look*, February 1, 1949.

Valentine, Sarah. *When I Was White: A Memoir*. New York: St. Martin's Press, 2019.

Ward, Gayle. *Crossing the Line: Racial Passing in 20th Century U.S. Literature and Culture*. Durham, NC: Duke University Press, 2000.

Weisenfeld, Judith. *Hollywood Be Thy Name: African American Religion in American Film, 1929–1949*. Berkeley, CA: University of California Press, 2007.

Wittern-Keller, Laura. *Freedom of the Screen: Legal Challenges to State Film Censorship, 1915–1981*. Frankfort, KY: University Press of Kentucky, 2008.

White, W. L. *Lost Boundaries*. Boston: Harcourt, Brace & World, Inc., 1947.

———. "Lost Boundaries." *Reader's Digest*, December 1947.

White, Walter. "On the Tragedy of the Color Line." *New York Times*, March 28, 1948.

Zolotow, Maurice. "Want to Be a Movie Star?" *The Saturday Evening Post*, March 1952.

Forty Acres and a Mule

Allen, William Francis, et al. *Slave Songs of the United States*. New York: A. Simpson & Co., 1867.

Ames, Mary. *From a New England Woman's Diary in Dixie in 1865*. Norwood, MA: The Plimpton Press, 1906.

Bentley, George R. *A History of the Freedmen's Bureau*. Philadelphia: University of Pennsylvania, 1955.

Botume, Elizabeth Hyde. *First Days Amongst the Contrabands*. Boston: Lee and Shepard, 1893.

Callahan, Allen Dwight. *The Talking Book: African Americans and the Bible*. New Haven, CT: Yale University Press, 2006.

Carpenter, John A. *Sword and Olive Branch: Oliver Otis Howard*. New York: Fordham University Press, 1999.

Charles Henry Howard Collection, George J. Mitchell Department of Special Collections & Archives, Bowdoin College Library, Brunswick, Maine.

Copeland, Roy W. "In the Beginning: Origins of African American Real Property Ownership in the United States." *Journal of Black Studies*, 44, no. 6 (September 2013).

Cox, LaWanda. "The Promise of Land for the Freedmen." *The Mississippi Valley Historical Review*, 45, no. 3 (December 1958).

Darden, Robert. *Nothing But Love in God's Water: Black Sacred Music from the Civil War to the Civil Rights Movement*. Philadephia: The Pennsylvania State University Press, 2014.

Drago, Edwin M. "How Sherman's March through Georgia Affected the Slaves." *The Georgia Historical Quarterly*, 57, no. 3 (Fall 1973).

Du Bois, W. E. B. *Black Reconstruction in America*. Boston: Harcourt, Brace and Company, 1935.

———. *The Souls of Black Folk*. Chicago: A. C. McClurg & Co., 1903.

"Edisto Island—The Freedmen—Gen. Howard's Recent Visit." *The Liberator*, December 1, 1865.

Egerton, Douglas R. *The Wars of Reconstruction*. London: Bloomsbury Press, 2014.

Eliot, Thomas D., Rep. Debating Reconstruction resolution and the Freedmen's Bureau. 39th Congress, 1st Session. *Congressional Globe*. Part 1, p. 517, January 30, 1866.

Epstein, Dena J. *Sinful Tunes and Spirituals: Black Folk Music to the Civil War*. Champaign, IL: University of Illinois Press, 1977.

Fellman, Michael. *Citizen Sherman*. New York: Random House, 1995.

Foner, Eric. *Forever Free: The Story of Emancipation and Reconstruction*. New York: Alfred A. Knopf, 2005.

———. *Reconstruction: America's Unfinished Revolution, 1863–1877*. Updated ed., New York: Harper Perennial, 2014.

Gordon-Reed, Annette. *Andrew Johnson*. Chicago and New York: Times Books, 2011.

Hahn, Steven. *Freedom: A Documentary History of Emancipation, 1861–1867 Series 3, Volume 1: Land and Labor, 1865*. Durham, NC: The University of North Carolina Press, 2008.

Harper, Matthew. *The End of Days: African American Religion and Politics in the Age of Emancipation*. Durham, NC: The University of North Carolina Press, 2016.

Howard, Oliver Otis. *Autobiography of Oliver Otis Howard*. Charlotte, NC, and New York: The Baker & Taylor Company, 1908.

James, Josef F. "Sherman at Savannah." *The Journal of Negro History*, 39, no. 2 (April 1954).

Johnson, Andrew, and Frank Moore. *Speeches of Andrew Johnson: President of the United States*. Boston: Little, Brown, and Co., 1866.

Langguth, A. J. *After Lincoln: How the North Won the Civil War and Lost the Peace*. New York: Simon & Schuster, 2014.

Letter from "E. B." *The Liberator*, December 15, 1865.

Levine, Lawrence W. *Black Culture and Black Consciousness*. Oxford: Oxford University Press, 1977.

Littwack, Leon F. *Been in the Storm So Long: The Aftermath of Slavery*. New York: Alfred A. Knopf, 1980.

McDonough, James Lee. *William Tecumseh Sherman: In the Service of My Country*. New York: W. W. Norton & Company, 2016.

McFeely, William S. *Yankee Stepfather: General O. O. Howard and the Freedmen*. New York: W. W. Norton & Company, 1994.

McNaughton, John Hugh. *Where is Our Moses?* Sheet music. Boston: Oliver Ditson & Co., 1866.

McPherson, Edward. *A Political Manual for 1866: Including a Classified*

Summary of the Important Executive, Legislative, and Politico-military Facts of the Period from President Johnson's Accession . . . to July 4, 1866. . . . Washington, DC: Philp & Solomons, 1866.

"Minutes of an Interview between the Colored Ministers and Church Officers at Savannah with the Secretary of War and Major-Gen. Sherman. Headquarters of Maj.-Gen. Sherman, City of Savannah, Ga., Jan. 12, 1865—8 P.M." *New-York Tribune*, February 13, 1865.

Nieman, Donald G. *To Set the Law in Motion: The Freedmen's Bureau and the Legal rights of Blacks, 1865–1868.* KTO Press, 1979.

Oliver Otis Howard Papers, George J. Mitchell Department of Special Collections & Archives, Bowdoin College Library, Brunswick, Maine.

Oubre, Claude F. *Forty Acres and a Mule: The Freedmen's Bureau and Black Land Ownership.* Baton Rouge, LA: Louisiana State University Press, 1978.

Raboteau, Albert J. *Slave Religion: The "Invisible Institution" in the Antebellum South.* Oxford: Oxford University Press, 1978.

Richardson, Heather Cox. *West from Appomattox: The Reconstruction of America after the Civil War.* New Haven, CT: Yale University Press, 2007.

Rose, Willie Lee. *Rehearsal for Reconstruction: The Port Royal Experiment.* 1964. Athens, GA: The University of Georgia Press, 1999.

Rowland Bailey Howard Papers, George J. Mitchell Department of Special Collections & Archives, Bowdoin College Library, Brunswick, Maine.

Schurz, Carl. *The Reminiscences of Carl Schurz.* Vol. 3. New York: The McClure Company, 1908.

Sharfstein, Daniel J. *Thunder in the Mountains: Chief Joseph, Oliver Otis Howard and the Nez Perce War.* New York: W. W. Norton & Co., 2017.

Sherman, William Tecumseh. *Memoirs of General William T. Sherman.* New York: D. Appleton and Company, 1875.

Simpson, Brooks D. *The Reconstruction Presidents.* Lawrence: KS: University Press of Kansas, 1998.

Small, Sandra E. "The Yankee Schoolmarm in Freedmen's Schools: An Analysis of Attitudes." *The Journal of Southern History*, 45, no. 3 (August 1979).

Stahr, Walter. *Stanton: Lincoln's War Secretary.* New York: Simon & Schuster, 2017.

Stewart, David O. *Impeached: The Trial of Andrew Johnson and the Fight for Lincoln's Legacy.* New York: Simon & Schuster, 2009.

Taylor, Susie King. *Reminiscences of My Life in Camp.* Susie King Taylor, 1902.

Tremain, Henry Edwin. *Two Days of War: A Gettysburg Narrative and Other Excursions.* New York: Bonnell, Silver and Bowers, 1905.

US Congress. House Committee on the Judiciary. *Impeachment Investigation: Testimony Taken Before the Judiciary Committee of the House of Representatives in the Investigation of the Charges Against Andrew Johnson.* 39th Congress, 2nd Session & 40th Congress, 1st Session, 1867.

Webster, Laura Josephine. *The Operation of the Freedmen's Bureau in South Carolina.* Northampton, MA: Department of History of Smith College, 1916.

Westwood, Howard C. "Sherman Marched—And Proclaimed 'Land for the Landless.'" *The South Carolina Historical Magazine,* 85, 1 (January 1984).

The Relief Canoes of 1638

Axtell, James. *Beyond 1492.* Oxford: Oxford University Press, 1992.

Baker, James W. *Thanksgiving: The Biography of an American Holiday,* Hanover, NH: University of New Hampshire Press, 2009.

Blake, Andrew F. "Sargent Apologizes for Official's Action." *The Boston Globe,* October 18, 1970.

Bradford, William, and Edward Winslow. *Mourt's Relation, or Journal of the Plantation at Plymouth* (1622). Boston: J. K. Wiggin, 1865.

Bruchac, Margaret M. "Reconsidering the English Settlement of Springfield, Massachusetts: Agawam Generosity and Colonial Violence." https://sites.google.com/view/springfieldagawam-landacknowl/home?authuser=2

———. "Revisiting Pocumtuck History in Deerfield: George Sheldon's Vanishing Indian Act." *Historical Journal of Massachusetts,* 39, nos. 1 and 2 (June 2011).

Bruchac, Margaret M., and Siobhan M. Hart. "Materiality and Autonomy in the Pocumtuck Homeland." *Archaeologies,* 8, no. 3 (December 2012).

Bruchac, Margaret M., and Peter Thomas. "Locating 'Wissatinnewag' in John Pynchon's Letter of 1663." *Historical Journal of Massachusetts,* 34, no. 1 (Winter 2006).

Calloway, Colin G., ed. *New Worlds for All: Indians, Europeans, and the Remaking of Early America*. Baltimore, MD: The Johns Hopkins University Press, 1997.

———. *After King Philip's War: Presence and Persistence in Indian New England*. Hanover, NH: University Press of New England, 1997.

Cameron, Catherine M., Paul Kelton, and Alan C. Swedlund, eds. *Beyond Germs: Native Depopulation in North America*. Tucson, AZ: University of Arizona Press, 2015.

Carr, Robert, and Andrew Blake. "Stage Plymouth Protest: Indians Take Over Mayflower II." *The Boston Globe*, November 27, 1970.

Cave, Alfred A. *The Pequot War*. Amherst, MA: University of Massachusetts Press, 1996.

Coombs, Linda. "First Thanksgiving." Talk at Boston City Hall, n.d. http://www.manyhoops.com/wampanoag-on-thanksgiving.html/

Cronon, William. *Changes in the Land: Indians, Colonists, and the Ecology of New England*. New York: Hill and Wang, 1983.

Drake, James D. *King Philip's War: Civil War in New England 1675–1676*. Amherst, MA: University of Massachusetts Press, 1999.

Finley, Ruth E. *The Lady of Godey's: Sarah Josepha Hale*. Philadelphia: J. B. Lippincott Company, 1931.

Fitzgerald, F. Scott. *The Great Gatsby*. New York: Charles Scribner's Sons, 1925.

Freeman, Michael. "Puritans and Pequots: The Question of Genocide." *The New England Quarterly*, 68, no. 2 (June 1995).

Gardner, Lion. Sachem Miantonomi's visit to Long Island. http://historymatters.gmu.edu/d/6227/

Grace, Catherine O'Neill, and Margaret M. Bruchac, et al. *1621: A New Look at Thanksgiving*. National Geographic Society, 2001.

Grandjean, Katherine A. "The Long Wake of the Pequot War." *Early American Studies*, 9, no. 2 (Spring 2011).

Green, Mason A. *Springfield 1636–1886: History of Town and City*. Springfield, MA: C. A. Nichols and Company, 1888.

Gura, Philip F. "'The Contagion of Corrupt Opinions' in Puritan Massachusetts: The Case of William Pynchon." *The William and Mary Quarterly*, 39, no. 3 (July 1982).

Hale, S. J. *Northwood: A Tale of New England*. Boston: Bowles & Dearborn, 1827.

Hale, Sarah Josepha. "Editor's Table." On Thanksgiving, 1855, 1857,

1858, 1859, 1860. http://www.uvm.edu/~hag/godey/shtable/shtable-thanks.html

Hobsbawm, Eric, ed. *The Invention of Tradition*. Cambridge, UK: Cambridge University Press, 1984.

Hodgson, Godfrey. *A Great and Godly Adventure: The Pilgrims and the Myth of the First Thanksgiving*. New York: Public Affairs, 2006.

Howe, Daniel Walker. *What Hath God Wrought: The Transformation of America, 1815–1848*. Oxford: Oxford University Press, 2007.

James, Wamsutta Frank. "Suppressed Speech." http://www.uaine.org/suppressed_speech.htm

Katz, Steven T. "The Pequot War Reconsidered." *The New England Quarterly*, 64, no. 2 (June 1991).

Lepore, Jill. *The Name of War: King Philip's War and the Origins of American Identity*. New York: Alfred A. Knopf, 1998.

Mansfield, Howard. "Four Centuries of King Philip's War" in *Turn & Jump: How Time & Place Fell Apart*. Camden, ME: DownEast Books, 2010.

———. "I Still Live." *Yankee*, November 2001.

———. "Pandemic Tells the True Story of the Pilgrims at Plymouth Rock." *Los Angeles Times*, November 25, 2020.

Martin, Lawrence. "The Genesis of Godey's Lady's Book." *The New England Quarterly*, 1, no. 1 (January 1928).

Mather, Cotton. *Magnalia Christi American: Or, the Ecclesiastical History of New-England, from Its First Planting, in the Year 1620, Unto the Year of Our Lord 1698*, Vol. 2. Thomas Robbins, 1853.

Means, Russell, and Marvin Wolf. *Where White Men Fear to Tread: The Autobiography of Russell Means*. New York: St. Martin's Publishing Group, 1995.

Melvion, Richard I. *New England Outpost: War and Society in Colonial Deerfield*. New York: W. W. Norton & Company, 1992.

Morrison, Samuel Eliot. "William Pynchon, the Founder of Springfield." *Proceedings of the Massachusetts Historical Society*. Third Series, Vol. 64, October 1930–June 1932.

Mott, Frank Luther. *A History of American Magazines: 1741–1850*. Cambridge, MA: Harvard University Press, 1938.

"Mourning Indians Dump Sand on Plymouth Rock." *New York Times*, November 27, 1970.

Oberg, Michael Leroy. "'We Are All the Sachems from East to West':

A New Look at Miantonomi's Campaign of Resistance." *The New England Quarterly*, 77, no. 3 (September 2004).

O'Brien, Jean M. *Firsting and Lasting: Writing Indians Out of Existence in New England*. Minneapolis, MN: University of Minnesota Press, 2010.

Peters, Ramona. "Beyond Vacationland: The Native American Cape Cod Story." Project 562. http://www.project562.com/blog/beyond-vacationland-the-native-american-cape-cod-story/

———. "How Should Thanksgiving Be Taught in the Schools?" *Canku Ota (Many Paths): An Online Newsletter Celebrating Native America*, December 2016. http://www.turtletrack.org

Pleck, Elizabeth. "The Making of the Domestic Occasion: The History of Thanksgiving in the United States." *Journal of Social History*, 32, no. 4 (Summer 1999).

Pocumtuck Valley Memorial Association. *History and Proceedings of the Pocumtuck Valley Memorial Association*, Vol. 2. The Association, 1890.

Powers, David M. *Damnable Heresy: William Pynchon, the Indians, and the First Book Banned (and Burned) in Boston*. Eugene, OR: Wipf and Stock Publishers, 2015.

Pynchon, William. "Letters of William Pynchon." *Proceedings of the Massachusetts Historical Society*. Third Series, Vol. 48, October 1914–June 1915.

Roth, Philip. "I Have Fallen in Love with American Names." *The New Yorker*, June 5, 2017.

Salisbury, Neal. *Manitou and Providence: Indians, Europeans, and the Making of New England, 1500–1643*. Oxford: Oxford University Press, 1982.

Sheldon, George. *A History of Deerfield, Massachusetts . . . With a Special Study of the Indian Wars in the Connecticut Valley*. Deerfield, MA: E. A. Hall & Co., 1895.

Silverman, David J. *This Land Is Their Land: The Wampanoag Indians, Plymouth Colony, and the Troubled History of Thanksgiving*. London: Bloomsbury Publishing, 2019.

Sommers, Joseph Michael. "Godey's Lady's Book: Sarah Hale and the Construction of Sentimental Nationalism." *College Literature*, 37, no. 3 (Summer 2010).

Tarbell, Ida. "The American Woman: Those Who Did Not Fight." *American Magazine*, Vol. 69, March 1910.

Taylor, William R. *Cavalier and Yankee: The Old South and American National Character* (1961). Oxford: Oxford University Press, 1993.

Thomas, Peter A. Correspondence with the author, February 6, 2020.

———. *In the Maelstrom of Change: The Indian Trade and Cultural Process in the Middle Connecticut River Valley, 1635–1665.* United States: Garland Publishing, Inc., 1990.

United American Indians of New England. "October 19, 1998 Settlement. Statement of United American Indians of New England on the dropping of charges against Plymouth defendants and settlement with Plymouth." http://www.uaine.org/settlement.htm

Wampanoag Indian Program. *Thanks, But No Thanks. Mirroring the Myth: Native Perspectives on Thanksgiving.* Plymouth, MA: Plimoth Plantation, September 9, 2000.

Ward, Kyle. *History in the Making.* New York: The New Press, 2006.

Webb, Stephen Saunders. *1676: The End of American Independence.* New York: Alfred A. Knopf, 1984.

Wills, Anne Blue. "Pilgrims and Progress: How Magazines Made Thanksgiving." *Church History*, 72, no. 1 (March 2003).

ACKNOWLEDGMENTS

For their insights into the Shakers, I thank: Charles "Bud" Thompson, Darryl Thompson, David Lamb, Renee Fox, Maggie Stier, June Sprigg, Jerry Grant, and Brad Fletcher.

I am indebted to the late Richard Merryman, author of the superb biography of Andrew Wyeth, for his incisive advice about writing about artists. I miss him.

More thanks are due than I can sum up to James and Beth Aponovich for all the hours discussing art and life over good meals, and in our travels in New Hampshire and Italy.

Thanks to Larry Benaquist, the Johnston family, and archivist Rodney Obien for their help on the Lost Boundaries chapter.

Thanks to Jody Simpson for research on historical music; historians Scott French, Peter Thomas, and James Garvin; Mount Washington Auto Road manager Howie Wemyss; New Hampshire Historical Society Library director Sarah Galligan; Dennis Northcott, associate archivist for Reference, Missouri Historical Society; Hancock Library director Amy Markus for retrieving a seemingly unending list of books through interlibrary loan; Library Services supervisor Robin Riley for her help navigating the Keene State College library during the pandemic; and Jane Eklund for her sharp editing.

As always, my deepest thanks to my wife and editor, the octopus whisperer, turtle wrangler, and caretaker of good creatures, Sy Montgomery.